# Casual Bead
# Elegance
## STITCH BY STITCH

**Kalmbach Books**
21027 Crossroads Circle
Waukesha, Wisconsin 53186
www.JewelryAndBeadingStore.com

Published in 2017
21 20 19 18 17    1 2 3 4 5

Manufactured in China

ISBN: 978-1-62700-312-4
EISBN: 978-1-62700-313-1


**Editor:** Erica Swanson
**Book Design:** Lisa Schroeder
**Technical Editor:** Dana Meredith
**Photographer:** William Zuback


**Library of Congress Control Number:** 2016943709

# Casual Bead Elegance
## STITCH BY STITCH

Eve Leder

KALMBACH BOOKS

Waukesha, Wisconsin

# Contents

# Introduction

Have you ever wanted to learn how to make beautiful beaded jewelry like the ones you've seen in the beading magazine on the news stand, but something keeps holding you back? I wrote this book to make learning to bead stitch (off the loom) more accessible and enjoyable. I tried to achieve these goals through development of the projects and the book format.

My approach combines two methods of learning: contextual and progressive. You'll get to make jewelry that you can be proud of while you are learning the stitches. Projects were designed to make understanding stitch construction easier. There are basically three categories of projects: *learn* (stitch introduction), *practice* (explore the stitch), and *apply* (expand your skills).

You should follow the projects in sequence: Learn, then practice, and apply. When I created each "learn" project, I tried to distill the stitch down to its simplest element. These easy projects provide the most detail about the basic technique. Your goal for each "learn" project is to develop an understanding of the thread path—or in other words—the stitch construction. The introductory project can also be used as reference if needed when working later projects of the same stitch.

The "practice" projects build upon what was learned from the first project. You'll develop a deeper understanding of the basic stitch and expand upon it. The detail level for new concepts (that build on the stitch) will be comparable to the "learn" projects. The "apply" project takes longer to complete than other projects and gives you the opportunity to expand what you learned and hopefully to have a sense of pride from seeing how you have progressed.

Before you buy the supplies, read the reference information found in the basics section at the front of the book. The reference material includes useful information on things like how to make the most of your beading budget and which beads can be substituted for each other.

It is my hope that as you work your way through the book, your view of the projects will change. Perhaps at the start your mindset is, "I'd love to make them, but I don't know if I can." As you gain knowledge and confidence, you might think, "I'd love to make them; they look a little bit challenging, but I am willing to give them a try." And, fingers crossed, once you have even more experience, you'll be thinking, "I'd love to make them and I am so proud that I tried because I did it!"

Happy Beading!
—Eve

# Basics

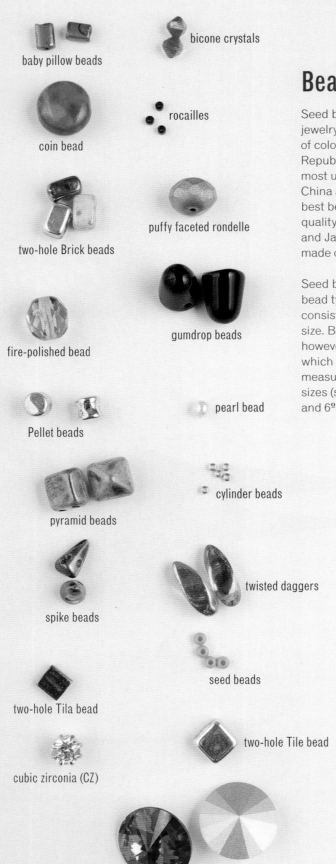

baby pillow beads

bicone crystals

coin bead

rocailles

two-hole Brick beads

puffy faceted rondelle

fire-polished bead

gumdrop beads

Pellet beads

pearl bead

pyramid beads

cylinder beads

spike beads

twisted daggers

seed beads

two-hole Tila bead

cubic zirconia (CZ)

two-hole Tile bead

rivolis

# Beads

Seed beads are the basic building block of stitched jewelry. They are widely available and come in a variety of colors. Most seed beads are made in Japan, the Czech Republic, and China. The beads made in Japan are the most uniform in size and shape, and the beads made in China are the least uniform in size and shape. For the best beading experience, I would spend a bit more to get quality beads. Czech beads tend to be sold by the hank and Japanese and Chinese are sold by the gram. A hank is made of 12 strands, folded in half into a bundle.

Seed beads are combined with a variety of specialty bead types and shapes. Be sure to buy beads that are consistent in terms of the outer dimension and the hole size. Bead packages are marked with a general size; however, in cheaper beads, there can be a lot of variation, which can compromise your results. Aught is a system of measurement for seed beads. The most common aught sizes (starting with the smallest) are 15º, 12º, 11º, 10º, 8º, and 6º. You'll see multiple sizes in this book.

## CONVERSION CHART

| MILLIMETER | AUGHT SIZING SCALE |
|---|---|
| 1.5mm | 15º |
| 2mm | 11º (10º would be okay too) |
| 3mm | 8º |

Have you ever gone clothes shopping and some garments in your size fit and others don't? This is because the dimension of a size can vary from country to country, from designer to designer, and sometimes even from style to style. The same thing can happen with beads; keep this in mind when buying materials for a project. For example, if a project requires a bead cap, then I would recommend waiting until it is finished to ensure that the bead cap will fit.

# Glossary

A **baby pillow bead** is a flattened cylinder shaped like a pillow.

A **bicone** is a shape created by putting the base of two triangles (cones) together. Swarovski is the most common supplier of bicone crystals.

**Coin beads** are Czech circle beads made from pressed glass. The ones used in this book have a diameter of 8mm and approximately 4mm in depth.

**Cylinder beads** are known for their uniform size and shape, as well as their large holes. These are ideal for stitches that require multiple thread passes or tidiness, like the peyote stitch. Two manufacturers of these beads are Miyuki, which make Delicas, and Toho, which makes Treasures and Aikos.

A **cubic zirconia (CZ)** is a synthetic crystal created to look like a diamond. It is prong set and comes in a square or round shape.

A **faceted puffy rondelle** is a type of rondelle. A rondelle is typically flat or disk-shaped. A facet is a cut surface. A faceted bead has many cuts. Puffy means it has more dimension than the standard rondelle.

**Fire-polished beads** are glass beads that are created to look like gemstones. They come in a variety of sizes, shapes, and finishes. This is a budget-friendly alternative to crystal beads.

A **gumdrop bead** looks like the candy for which it is named. The hole is by the flat base.

**Pearl beads** are created to look like real pearls. If you want to create high-end jewelry, buy glass pearls or freshwater pearls, not plastic pearls.

**Pellet beads** are 4x6mm beads from Czech Preciosa that are shaped like a spool of thread with a pinched center.

**Pyramid beads** are a combination of a square bead with a triangle bead. You may see it referred to as a Pyramid Beadstud, Pyramid, or Beadstud. To me, the 6mm size bead are shaped more like a Pyramid found in Egypt then the larger ones (8mm and 12mm).

A **rivoli** is a round, faceted crystal with a pointed front and back.

A **rocaille** is small seed bead, sized at 15º.

**Spike beads** are shaped like a cone with a pointed top and a flat bottom. The hole is located near the flat bottom.

**Two-hole Brick beads** are 6x3x3mm rectangular pressed glass beads. They are part of the CzechMates series. Substitute with a Half-Tila, if desired.

A **two-hole Tila bead** is a square bead from Miyuki that is 5x5x1.9mm. It can be substituted for a Tile bead. Tilas also come in a half-sized version called half-Tila.

A **two-hole Tile bead** is a two-hole square bead similar to the Tila bead. They are part of the CzechMates series.

A **twisted dagger** is a Czech pressed glass bead shaped like a dagger. The shape of it reminds me of the light bulbs used for chandeliers. The bead is 6x12x4mm.

## SEED BEED FINISHES

AB is short for Aurora Borealis. The name comes from the northern lights. If AB follows the color, then a finish was applied to the surface, making it iridescent.

Ceylon, when it precedes the color name of a bead, indicates the addition of a luster coating or the inside coloring of an opalescent bead. It creates a pearl-like appearance.

Iris is a finish similar to AB. It is iridescent, but iris is darker and has a shorter color spectrum.

end cap

box clasp

# Findings

These are metal components used to connect and/or assemble jewelry. Some examples are: jump rings, clasps, bails, earring wires, and charms.

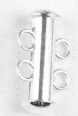

multistrand clasp

toggle clasp

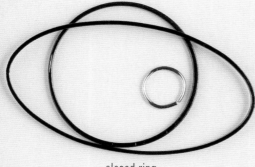

closed ring

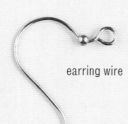

earring wire

jump rings

pin back

ribbon end

# COMMON FINDINGS

An **end cap** (cord cap) is a domed cylinder, often with a loop. It is typically used with three-dimensional stitches such as cubic right-angle weave and tubular herringbone. It is glued into place and acts as a transition from the beadwork to the clasp.

**Box clasps** have a tab which is inserted into a decorative frame or box. Some styles come with safety latches or safety chains, which prevent the wedge-shaped tab from pulling out and the jewelry from dropping off. Some styles are accented with gemstones, enamel, or inlay work.

**Multistrand clasps** secure jewelry with two, three, four, or more strands.

**Slide-lock clasps** consist of a set of tubes, one of which slides inside the other and locks into place. The bar style of these multi-strand clasps holds an almost unlimited number of strands of chain, cord, beading wire, or thread.

**A toggle clasp** is comprised of a ring and bar.

A **closed ring** (link) is a solid shape that can be used as a link or a stitch base that can be worked off of like in the first butterfly project. It comes in different sizes and shapes.

An **earring wire** comes in various styles: hoop, French hook, post, and kidney.

A **jump ring** is a circle of wire that is either soldered or cut so you can open and close the circle. It is used to connect jewelry components together. Jump rings range in size and thickness (also called *gauge*). The higher the gauge, the thinner the wire.

A **pin back** has a hinged arm on one end and a hook on the other end. In this book, it is sewed onto the beadwork to create a pin.

A **ribbon end** is used to finish off ribbon and beadwork in order to attach it to a clasp. It is a folded over rectangle with loop on its folded edge and teeth along the edges to grip the beadwork.

# Thread

The beading thread used for the projects in this book is similar to fishing line. For beginners, I recommend buying a light and dark thread with a 6 lb. strength and with a diameter of .008" (.2mm), or .006" if you can't find the .008". Two brands that you are likely to find and can be used interchangeably are Fireline and WildFire. (WildFire thread tends to be thicker than Fireline.)

# Color Ideas

Color selection can be overwhelming. You might not know off the top of your head what colors you like or which colors go together. If you are not sure, take a look at your wardrobe to see what colors you tend to favor (or page through this book to see which pieces or versions of the projects appeal to you). Deciding which colors go together can be challenging—especially when buying online. I find doing an internet search to see what others have done helpful. For example, you could search Pinterest for beaded jewelry in a specific color.

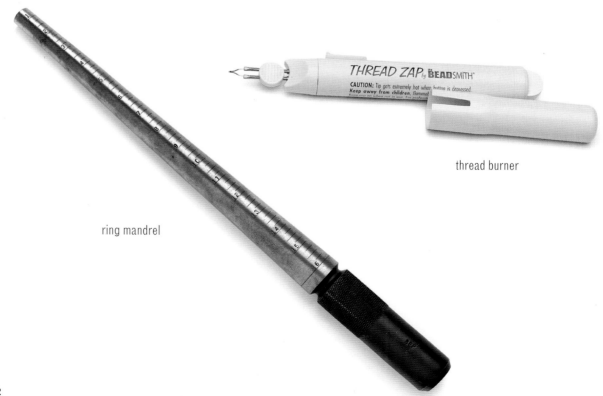

bentnose pliers

# Tools

I recommend a **big-eye beading needle** because it is easy to thread and works well with a variety of beading thread. Its large eye spans almost the entire length of the needle. It comes in two sizes: 2½" and 4". The 2½" works well for the projects in this book, but you can also use the 4". I've also used a 2½" collapsible eye needle (in a thin size). If the holes in a small bead (15º) are not consistent, you can still use the beads with this needle. However, the needle bends easily and either limits how long it is usable or really slows down the beading process.

Choose a pair of **scissors** that are small, sharp, and have a pointed end, such as an embroiderer's scissors. This will help you work in small spaces and cut your thread close to the work.

Use a **flexible tape measure or standard ruler** to size your work.

A **bead mat** is an approximately 9"x12" piece of fabric that feels like velour or velvet and it stops your beads from rolling off the table. You can buy one at a craft or bead store. You could also make one yourself: Select a fabric with texture that will prevent your beads from rolling without getting lost in thick pile.

**Roundnose pliers** have a smooth, round, and conical working surface. They are used for making loops. Round-nose pliers are also helpful for closing a gap in an earring wire or jump ring.

The working surface of **chainnose** or **flatnose pliers** is smooth, flat, and in the case of chainnose pliers, tapers to a point. These pliers are used for gripping and opening/closing loops and jump rings.

With **bentnose pliers**, the working surface and use is similar to that of chainnose pliers. Its pointed end is bent, which makes it easier to work in small spaces.

ring mandrel

thread burner

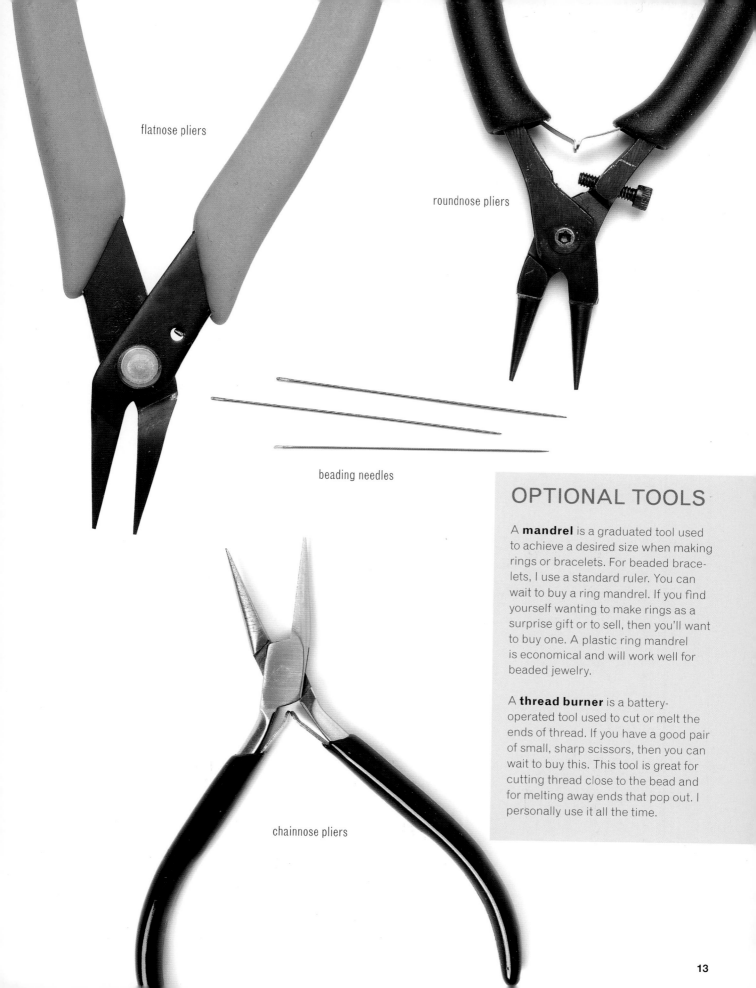

flatnose pliers

roundnose pliers

beading needles

chainnose pliers

## OPTIONAL TOOLS

A **mandrel** is a graduated tool used to achieve a desired size when making rings or bracelets. For beaded bracelets, I use a standard ruler. You can wait to buy a ring mandrel. If you find yourself wanting to make rings as a surprise gift or to sell, then you'll want to buy one. A plastic ring mandrel is economical and will work well for beaded jewelry.

A **thread burner** is a battery-operated tool used to cut or melt the ends of thread. If you have a good pair of small, sharp scissors, then you can wait to buy this. This tool is great for cutting thread close to the bead and for melting away ends that pop out. I personally use it all the time.

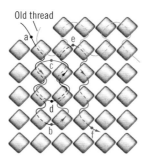

Old thread

adding a thread

half-hitch knot

square knot

stopper bead

# Before You Begin

There are some techniques and terms I will use throughout the book as I demonstrate new stitches. Review these basics before starting a project.

**Adding thread:** To add a thread, sew into the beadwork several rows prior to the point where the last bead was added. Weave through the beadwork following the thread path of the stitch. Tie a few half-hitch knots between the beads, and exit where the last stitch ended.

**Half-hitch knot:** Pass the needle under the thread between two beads. A loop will form as you pull the thread through. Cross back over the thread between the beads, sew through the loop, and pull gently to draw the knot into the beadwork.

**Square knot:** Cross the left-hand end of the thread over the right, and then under and back up. Cross the end that is now on the right over the left, go through the loop, and pull both ends to tighten.

**Starter bead:** A started bead is the bead the thread is exiting at the start of a step.

**Step up:** This is how you finish a round and position yourself to start the next row. You'll most likely find this term when working in a circular or tubular version of peyote, netting, or herringbone stitches. Instead of adding a bead, you are weaving the thread through the beads so that it is exiting the first bead added in the round.

**Stopper (or stop) bead:** A temporary bead used to prevent the other beads from falling off the thread is called a *stop bead*. Choose a bead that is distinctly different from the beads in your project. String the stopper bead, and sew through it again in the same direction. If desired, sew through it one more time for added security.

**Tail:** This is the thread that is below the first bead picked up. If a specific length is not mentioned, then leave a tail long enough to hold in your non-working hand to maintain tension and to be able to weave in at the end. Additionally, I often leave a tail to use for finishing off a piece of jewelry, like attaching a clasp.

**Weave through the beads or beadwork:** When you are instructed to "weave through the beads," you are passing your needle through the existing beadwork so you exit in a different spot. In order to keep thread hidden in the final piece, follow the thread path used to work the stitch.

**Working thread:** The working thread is the thread that is between a bead you picked up and the needle.

# Ladder Stitch

# Faux Circular Brick Stitch Earrings

The name of the stitch captures its essence: It is easy to compare the rungs of a ladder to the beads worked in the ladder stitch. When the stitch is done correctly, the beads are positioned neatly, parallel to each other. Your introduction to the stitch is the simplest version that uses only one bead type and is worked one bead at a time after the first pair.

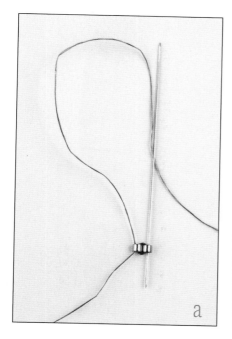

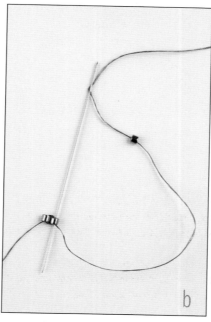

## MAKE THE EARRINGS

**1 |** Thread a needle on 2½' of thread. Pick up 2A. Pass the needle up through the bottom of the first bead, pulling tight, and down through the top of the second. Pass through the beads again, making sure to work with a tight tension and to create a firm base **(photo a)**. The holes of the beads should be facing you and their sides should be flush against each other.

**2 | Add five beads, one at a time:** Pick up 1A. Pass the needle through the top of the prior bead and up through the bottom of the bead just added. The thread path will alternate for each stitch **(photo b)**. When you add the next bead, the needle will go through the bottom of the previous bead. Work until you have a total of 7A. Make sure your strip of beads has a flat top and bottom edge, and don't let the beads get twisted.

## MATERIALS

- **36** 10º cylinder beads (bead A)
- **2** 8mm fire-polished beads (bead B)
- **26** 3mm glass pearls (bead C)
- 1g 10º Czech seed beads (bead D)
- **12** 4mm fire-polished beads (bead E)
- pair of earring wires
- beading thread, diameter 00.20 (.008")

## TOOLS

- scissors
- big-eye needle

**TIP:** *While working this stitch, keep a close eye on the beads to be sure they don't get twisted. I chose a large 10º cylinder bead because it is consistent in size and shape, which makes it easy to see if your beads are lining up.*

## Tail Terminology

*A tail is the thread that lies below the first bead picked up. If a specific length is not mentioned, then leave a tail long enough to hold in your non-working hand to maintain tension and to be able to weave in at the end. I often leave a long tail to use for attaching a clasp or another finding.*

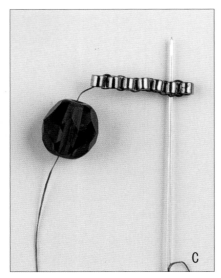 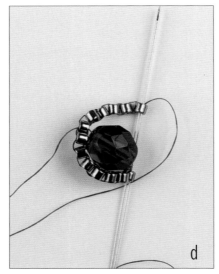 

**3 | Attach the ladder strip to the center bead:** Pick up 1B. Make sure the ladder stitch beads lie flat against the center bead. Pass the needle out through the second A picked up and back in by passing through the first A picked up **(photo c)**. Finish attaching the strip by passing through the B and back out through the seventh bead in the strip.

**4 |** Pick up the eighth A. Pass the needle up through the bottom of the seventh bead and down through the eighth A. Continue working until you have worked a total of 13 As.

**5 | Connect the ends of the ladder stitch strip:** Pass the needle down through the first A and up through the last A, following the same path as when you added a bead.  Make sure the beads are tidy and the strip you are connecting is not twisted. Repeat the path three times or until the beads are secure **(photo d)**.

**6 | Start embellishing:** Pick up 1C and 1D. Pass

back down through the B and the A below. Pass up through the next A. Apply this embellishment a total of 13 times **(photo e)**. After the last embellishment, pass up through the next A, C, and D. Take care not to twist D.

**7 | Attach the earring wire:** Pick up the earring wire. Pass the needle through the next D and down through the C and A below it. Complete the circuit by passing up through the starting units A and C. Then, pass through D. Repeat the thread path until secure. End with the thread exiting the second D **(photo f)**.

**8 | Finish embellishing:** [Pick up 1E and pass through the next D. Pick up 1A and pass through the next D.] Repeat the instructions between the brackets **(photo g)** three times. Pick up 1A and pass through the next D. Repeat the process using the following bead pattern: 1E, 1A, 1E, 1A, and 1E. (This makes a total of 6E and 6A added.) Weave in the ends and trim.

**9 |** Repeat to make a second earring.

# *Victorian Romance Ring*

## MATERIALS

- **36–51** 2mm Japanese seed beads (bead A)

- **4** two-hole Brick beads (bead B)

- **4** 11º Czech seed beads (bead C)

- **1** 8mm two-hole Pyramid bead (bead D)

- **6** 3mm Japanese seed beads (bead E)

- beading thread, diameter 00.20 (.008")

## TOOLS

- scissors

- big-eye needle

In the first project, you learned the thread path of the ladder stitch using one bead per stitch. In this project, you'll practice the technique using three beads per stitch. (You'll notice the thread path doesn't change just because you are picking up multiple seed beads per stitch.) This piece also incorporates a different bead type, one with multiple holes for an added twist.

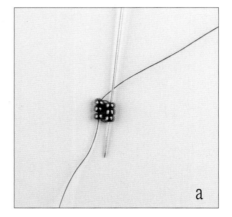
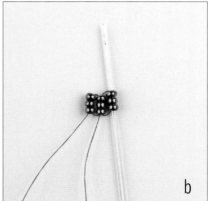

### MAKE THE RING

**1 | Start the ring band using ladder stitch:**
Thread a needle on 3' of thread. Pick up 6A, leaving a tail long enough to weave into your beadwork at the end. Pass through all the beads again to form two columns of three beads **(photo a)**. Repeat the path two more times to create a solid base for the ring band.

**2 |** Pick up 3A. Pass down through the last 3A in the previous step and then up through the 3A just picked up **(photo b)**. Continue working in ladder stitch, picking up 3A at a time, until you have a total of six columns of three beads.

**3 | Add a Brick bead and seed bead unit:** Pick up 1B and 3A. Pass through the second hole of the B, the 3A of the prior stitch, the first hole of the B, and the 3A added in this step **(photo c)**.

**4 |** Repeat step 3.

**NOTE:** *In these instructions, the sides of the Pyramid bead with the holes are referred to as the "top" and "bottom."*

**5 | Add a focal component:** Pick up 1C, 1D, and 1C. Pass through the 3A in the previous step and the beads picked up in this step. Retrace the thread path a couple of times or until secure, ending by exiting the D.

**6 | Frame the top and bottom of the focal bead:** Pick up 3E and pass through the second hole of the D. Pick up 3E and pass the needle through the next hole of the D. Reinforce the top and bottom frame by passing through all 6E added in this step until secure. The thread should be exiting the second hole of the D.

**7 | Start the other side of the ring band:** Pick up 1C, 3A, and 1C. Pass through the D and the beads picked up in this step. Retrace the thread path until secure. The thread should be exiting an A before the C.

**8 |** Repeat step 3 twice.

**9 |** Continue working in ladder stitch until you reach the desired ring size.

**10 | Sew the band ends together:** Pass through the very first 3A picked up and through the last 3A stitch. Retrace the thread path until secure **(photo d)**. Reinforce the stitches, if necessary, following the same path. Weave in the thread ends and trim.

c

d

# *Dream's Doorway Bracelet*

With this project, you'll get to continue to explore the versatility of this basic stitch. The right materials can add complexity and elevate something basic into something special. The bracelet's design is elevated by the variety of bead types, such as baby pillow beads, Tila beads, and seed beads.

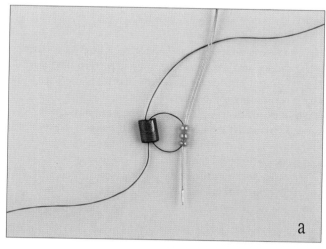

a

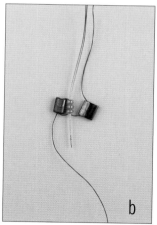

b

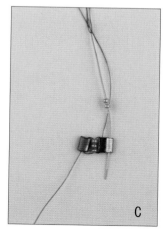

c

## MATERIALS

*The bracelet is 7¼" long, including the clasp.*

- hank 10º Czech seed beads (bead A)

- 2–3g 2mm Japanese seed beads (bead B)

- 2–3g 3mm Japanese seed beads (bead C)

- **37** 3x5mm baby pillow beads (bead D)

- **12** Tila beads (bead E)

- toggle clasp

- beading thread, diameter 00.20 (.008")

## TOOLS
- scissors

- big-eye needle

## CREATE THE BASE TILA UNITS

**1 |** Thread a needle on 4' of thread. Pick up 1D and 3A, leaving a 12" tail. Pass through all of the beads again **(photo a)**.

**2 |** Pick up 1E. Pass through 3A from step 1 **(photo b)** and the same hole of the E.

**3 |** Pick up 2A. Pass through the next hole of the E **(photo c)**.

**4** | Pick up 2A. Pass through the first hole of the E, across through the 2A, and through the second hole of the E **(photo d)**.

**5** | Pick up 3A. Pass through the E and through the beads just picked up **(photo e)**.

**6** | **Fill in the corners:** Pick up 1C and pass through the next group of As. Repeat to fill all four corners.

**7** | Pick up 1D. Pass through the closest 3A and the D you just added. You have completed one Tila bead unit.

**8** | Repeat steps 2–7 until you have achieved the desired length. The bracelet shown has 12 Tila units.

## FINISH THE TILA UNITS

**9** | Pick up 1B and pass through the next C. Pick up 1D and pass through the next C. Pick up 1B and pass through the next D. Pick up 1B and pass through the next C. Pick up 1D and pass through the next C. Pick up 1B and pass through the next D. Continue in the same direction and weave the thread around through the beads on the outside edge. End with the thread exiting the D that is shared with the next Tila unit. Repeat step 9 with the remaining Tila base units.

**10** | **Attach the clasp:** The thread should be exiting the D on the end. Pick up 7B and pass through the loop of the bar end of the clasp and the last 2B picked up. Pick up 5B. Complete the circuit by passing through the D again. Retrace the thread path several times until secure **(photo f)**. The ring side of the clasp is attached the same way, but with fewer beads picked up: Pick up 5B, pass through the last 2B added, and pick up 3B before completing the circuit. Repeat the thread path several times until secure. Weave the thread ends in and trim.

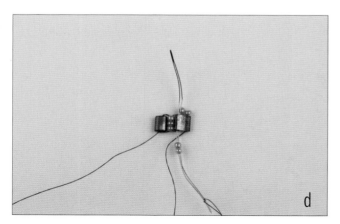

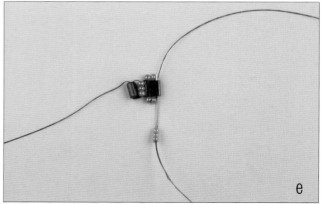

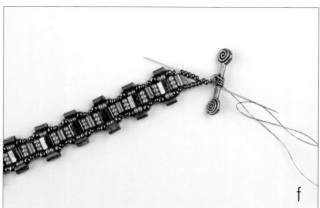

# Right-Angle Weave

Gumdrop Ring

The basic concept of the right-angle weave (RAW) stitch is simple. First, pick up four beads. Then, complete the stitch by passing through the beads again from the same side that you picked them up from originally. The resulting shape is square. A square is made of right angles—hence, the name of the stitch. Using the right-angle weave stitch to create the ring band is the simplest application of the stitch. As you create the band, try to be aware that the thread path direction alternates between clockwise and counterclockwise. Understanding this point will help make working multiple rows of the stitch seem more intuitive.

## MATERIALS

- 1g 11º Japanese seed beads (bead A)

- 1g 2mm Japanese seed beads (bead B)

- **6** 3mm Japanese seed beads (bead C)

- **6** 5x8mm spike beads (bead D)

- **1** 7x10mm gumdrop bead (bead E)

- beading thread, diameter 00.20 (.008")

## TOOLS

- big-eye needle

- scissors

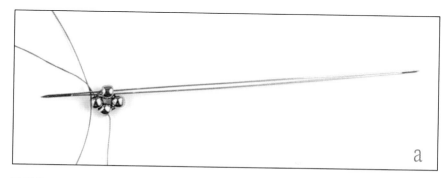

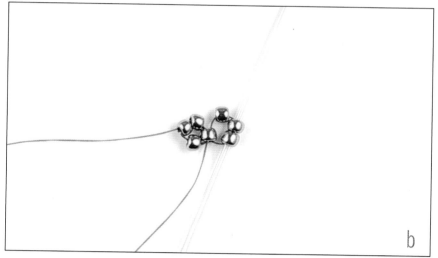

## MAKE THE RING

**1 | Start the right-angle weave band:** Thread a needle on 3' of thread, and pick up 4A, leaving a 6" tail. Pass through all of the beads picked up and the first 3A again **(photo a)**. This is the first right-angle weave stitch. Notice how it makes a square shape.

**2 |** Pick up 3A. Pass through the starter bead, the bead the thread was exiting at the start of this step, and the first 2A picked up **(photo b)**. Repeat four more times (this makes a total of six stitches).

c

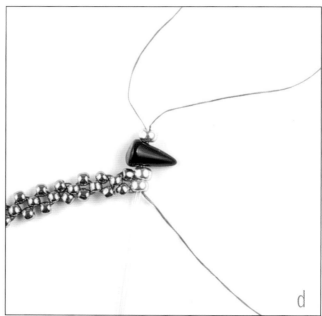

d

**3 | Start the frame of the focal bead:** Pick up 1A, 1C, and 1A **(photo c)**. Pass through the starter bead and the first two beads picked up. Pick up 1C, 1D, and 1C **(photo d)**. Pass through the starter bead and the first two beads picked up. Pick up 1D, 2A, 1E, 2A, and 1D **(photo e)**. Pass through the starter bead, 1D, 2A, and 1E. Make sure the tops of the spike beads and the gumdrop are facing in the same direction.

**4 |** Pick up 2A, 3D, and 2A. Pass through the E and the beads added again **(photo f)**.

**5 |** Pass through all the beads surrounding the E a couple of times to close the gap between the pairs of As above and below the E. (The thread will be exiting the middle spike of the second group of 3D.)

# Reinforcing Stitches

Putting on and taking off a ring can strain it, so reinforcing it with lots of thread is a good idea. Normally, I recommend waiting until you are completely done with a project before reinforcing because you are working with small beads. Reinforcing too early might mean you won't be able to pass the needle through a bead again because the hole will be filled with thread. (This is important if you are going to add an embellishment at a spot later on in the design.) However, you might want to consider a second pass through as you complete each stitch. Reinforcing stitches will bring the beads closer together, so you may need to work additional stitches to reach the desired size.

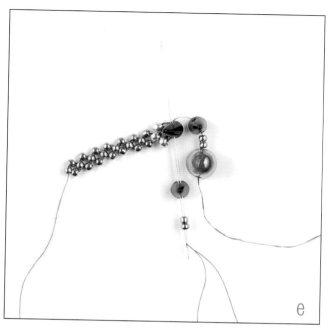

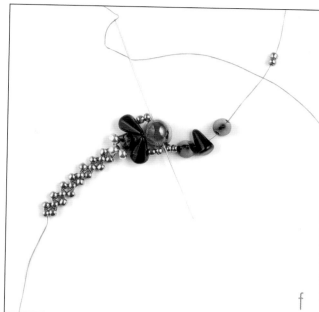

**6 | Close the frame of the focal bead:** Pick up 3C. Pass through the spike and the first 2C picked up.

**7 |** Continue working the ring band as in step 2. Using As, continue working the right-angle weave stitch until the band is the desired length to fit your finger.

**8 | Connect the band ends to form the ring:** Pick up 1A, pass through the corresponding bead from the first stitch, pick up 1A, and pass through the starter bead **(photo g)**. Repeat the path until the thread is secure.

**9 |** Embellish the top and bottom edge of the band by filling in the spaces with seed beads: Pick up a B and pass through the next outside edge bead. Repeat to fill in all the spaces on the top and bottom band **(photo h)**.

**10 |** If reinforcing stitches, make sure the needle follows the original thread path to avoid letting the thread show. Weave the thread ends in and trim.

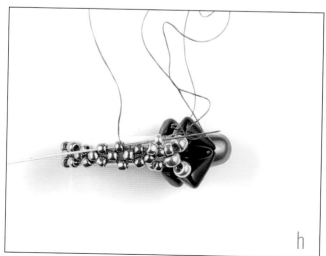

# Racing Stripe Earrings

While making this project, you'll practice and expand upon what you learned about right-angle weave (RAW). The only difference between working the center column of the earring versus working the ring band is that you will now be using two different bead pairs. Your understanding of RAW will expand as you create the two outside columns of the earrings. The alternating thread path direction will come into play as you create the two outside columns.

## Stitch Insight

The first stitch path variation comes when you work the first stitch on the side columns. It is worked off a side bead (shown in silver) instead of a top bead. The remaining stitches are different from previous stiches because two beads are picked up and the thread path isn't exactly the same. Different colored beads for the outside edge will act as a direction/color check.

### MATERIALS

- 1g 2mm Japanese seed beads (bead A)

- 1g 11° cylinder beads (bead B)

- **18** 3mm bicone crystals (bead C)

- beading thread, diameter 00.20 (.008")

- pair of earring wires

**NOTE:** *Cylinder beads are consistent in size and shape, which helps create a clean outside edge.*

### TOOLS

- scissors

- big-eye needle

**NOTE:** *The starter bead refers to the bead the thread is exiting at the start of a step.*

## STITCH THE CENTER COLUMN

**NOTE:** *Work using Cs and As. With the first unit, the needle path is in clockwise movement; with the second unit, the path is counter-clockwise; and so on.*

**1 | Make the first stitch, unit 1:** Thread a needle on 3' of thread. Pick up 1C, 1A, 1C, and 1A. Form a four-bead unit by passing through all the beads two times and then through the first three beads. The needle should be exiting the top C (opposite the first C picked up).

**2 | Make the second stitch, unit 2:** To create the second four-bead unit, pick up only three beads (the second unit shares a crystal with the first unit). Pick up 1A, 1C, and 1A. Pass through the starter bead and the first two beads picked up.

**3 | Work four more stitches:** Repeat step 2 four more times (see note regarding needle path). There should be a total of 7C in the middle column. After you have completed the 6th unit, going the same direction, weave the needle through so it exits a side A. The thread should be exiting the top of the A and away from you. Orient the piece so the needle is on the top right **(photo a)**.

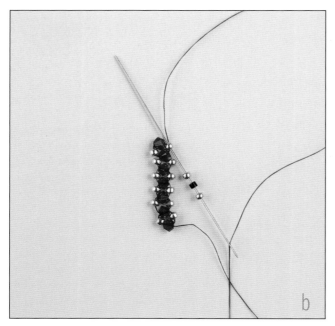

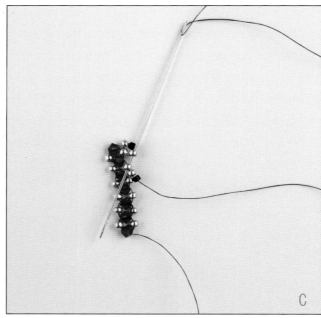

## STITCH THE RIGHT-SIDE COLUMN

**NOTE:** *Work using As and Bs. The thread path of the first stitch of the side column is clockwise. This is due to the orientation direction given in step 3. Stitches that have a clockwise thread path have an extra step in order to be in the right position for the next stitch. You will pass through the next available side bead from the center column.*

**4 | Make the first stitch, unit 1:** The first side column unit is worked like the second unit in the first column. The difference is that it shares a side A instead of a top C. Pick up 1A, 1B, and 1A. Pass the needle clockwise through the starter bead (side center A), the beads you just picked up, and the next available bead from the center column (side A) **(photo b)**.

**5| Make the second stitch, unit 2:** The second side column unit only requires the addition of two beads. It shares the A from the unit above and the A from the center column. Pick up 1A and 1B. Pass the needle counter-clockwise through the above A, the starter bead (side center A), and the A you just picked up **(photo c)**.

**6 | Make the third stitch, unit 3:** Pick up 1B and 1A. Pass the needle in a clockwise direction through the center column A, the A from the previous stitch, the two beads added in this step, and the next available bead from the center column.

**7 |** Finish the column by repeating steps 5, 6, and 5. After you complete the sixth stitch, weave the thread into position to work the second column. Going in the same direction, pass through the last B you picked up, the A above, and the center A (the starter bead). Then pass through the end C and the next A.

**8 |** Re-orient the piece so you are working on the top right-hand side. Flip the beads so the last stitch worked is now on the top and on the left side.

## SECOND-SIDE COLUMN

**NOTE:** *Work using As and Bs.*

**9 | Make the first stitch, unit 1:** Pick up 1A, 1B, and 1A. Pass the needle counter-clockwise through the starter bead (side center A) and the first A picked up.

**10 | Make the second stitch, unit 2:** Pick up 1B and 1A. Pass the needle clockwise through the center column A, the A from the previous stitch, the beads just added, and the next available A from the center column.

**11 | Make the third stitch, unit 3:** Pick up 1A and 1B. Pass the needle counter-clockwise through the above A, the starter bead (side center A), and the A you just picked up.

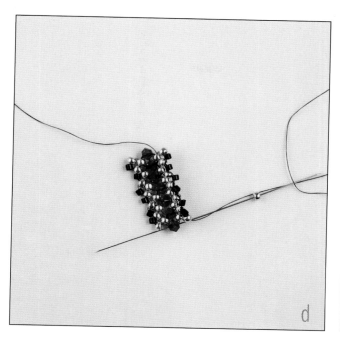

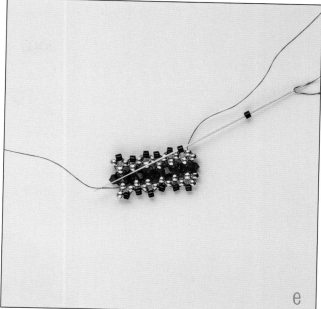

**12** | Finish the column by repeating steps 10, 11, and 10. Reinforce the last stitch by repeating the thread path. The thread should be exiting the bottom A.

## FILL IN THE OUTER EDGE

**NOTE:** *The open spaces along the outside edge are filled in with the same bead type: B. The open spaces at the top and bottom are filled in with As.*

**13** | Pick up 1A and pass through the next C **(photo d)**. Pick up 1A and pass through the next A and B. Finish off the side edge by filling in the spaces between the Bs. Pick up 1B and pass through the next B **(photo e)**. Continue adding Bs until you have added a total of 5B. Then pass through the next A.

**14** | Repeat the previous step. Weave the thread so it is exiting the closest crystal on an outside edge.

## ATTACH THE EARRING WIRE

**15** | Pick up 1C, an earring wire, and 1C. Pass through the starting crystal and first crystal picked up. Pick up 1A, pass through the earring wire, pick up 1A, and pass through the next 2C. Retrace the thread path until secure **(photo f)**. If necessary, reinforce the stiches by following the original needle path. Weave the thread ends in and trim.

In the third right-angle weave project, you'll apply what you learned to create this bracelet that gives the illusion the links were made from hammered metal. The secret to the illusion is using beads of different shapes. The reflective surface of the different shaped beads vary due to the cuts required to create the shapes.

## BLOCK (MAKE 5)

**NOTE:** *Work steps 1–7 using Bs.*

### ROW 1

**1 | Make Unit 1:** Thread a needle on 2½' of thread. Pick up 4B, leaving an 8" tail. Form a ring by passing through all the beads two times and then through the first three beads. The needle should be exiting the top bead.

**2 | Make Unit 2:** Pick up 3B. Pass through the starter bead (the bead the thread was exiting at the start of the step) and the first two beads picked up.

**3 |** Repeat step 2.

### ROW 2

**4 | Add a new row:** Weave the thread so it is exiting from the top edge of a side bead. Pick up 3B. Pass the needle clockwise through the starter bead, the beads you just picked up, and the next available bead from the first row.

**5 |** Pick up 2B. Pass the needle counter-clockwise through the bead above from the prior unit, the starter bead, and the first B picked up in this step.

**6 |** Work the last stitch of row 2. Weave the thread so it is exiting a side bead (from the open edge).

### ROW 3

**7 |** Work the third row of the right-angle stitch. The needle should be exiting from an outside edge bead.

## ASSEMBLE

### JOIN THE BLOCKS

**8 |** Pick up 1A, 1C, and 1A. Pass through the corresponding bead of the block being attached. Pick up 1A, pass through the second hole in the C, pick up 1A, and pass through the starter bead **(photo a)**. Retrace the thread path several times until secure. Weave the thread to the third bead on the same side. Repeat the joining process with the remaining blocks.

## MATERIALS

*The bracelet is 7" long, including the clasp.*

- 3g 8º Japanese seed beads (bead A)

- **120** 4mm fire-polished beads in assorted shapes (bead B)

- **8** 8mm Pyramid beads (bead C)

- beading thread, diameter 00.20 (.008")

- 16mm two-strand clasp

## TOOLS
- scissors

- big-eye needle

**NOTE:** *For the first unit, the needle follows a clockwise path. For the second unit, the path is counter-clockwise, and so on.*

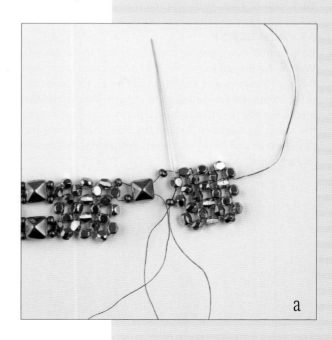

a

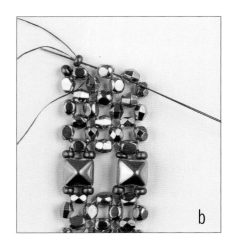
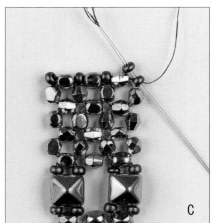
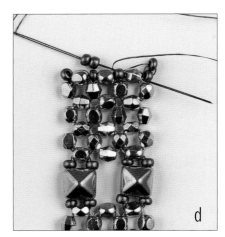

b

c

d

## FINISH OFF ENDS

**9 |** The thread should be exiting a side bead of a corner unit. Pick up 1A and pass through the closest B. Repeat a total of three times **(photo b)**. Pick up 1A, and pass down through the B below it. Continue passing through the remaining beads that make up that stitch and the bead just added.

**10 |** [Pick up 1A. Pass through the A below and through the bead just picked up **(photo c)**. Pick up 2A, and pass through the B below and two beads picked up **(photo d)**.] Repeat the instructions between the brackets three times. Pick up 1A, and pass through the bead below and the one just picked up.

**11 |** Pick up 1A. Pass through the A below and the one just picked up. Repeat the stitch to the end of the row.

**12 |** Repeat steps 9–11 on the other end of the bracelet.

## ATTACH CLASP

**13 |** Center one clasp half at one end of the bracelet. Weave the thread to the bead below a clasp loop. Pass through the loop and back into the bead. Retrace the thread path several times until secure. Weave the thread so the needle is exiting a bead below the second loop of the clasp, and repeat. Attach the other half of the clasp to the other end of the bracelet. Weave the thread ends in and trim.

# Design Insight

This project epitomizes my design process, which focuses on an organic approach to design. Some people might call this trial and error.

The first part of the process is material selection. I don't know if there is a word that means visually deafening. If there were such a word, then it would be defined as being overwhelmed by the process of selecting beads from a bead store. Whenever I notice someone experiencing this, I tell them to close their eyes and to think about what they remember. We may see everything, but we only actively remember based on our subconscious selection process. I think our subconscious mind's filter comes from a combination of our nature and our experience. I tend to remember the color that appeals to me most at a point in time.

The second part of the process is looking at the materials and trying to imagine what they should become. I always think it is weird to say the materials speak to me, but it seems to be the truth. I know there are some designers who sketch out their design first, but my design process is much more organic. This is especially true for three-dimensional mediums like beading. I did buy these beads thinking that I would try using them in a tubular herringbone stitch design. They turned out to be too big for this stich. However, when worked in right-angle weave stitch, the beads looked like a chain made of hammered metal. I realized this was the result of using different bead cuts in the same color. Not using the same bead shape meant the light would be absorbed and reflected in such a way as to give the appearance of a hammered metal chain.

# Cubic Right-Angle Weave

# Burned Gold and Topaz Earrings

The cubic right-angle weave stitch (CRAW) is an advanced version of the right-angle weave stitch. I highly recommend you work through the projects from the (basic) right-angle weave (RAW) stitch prior to starting this project. To me, the basic essence of the RAW stitch could be described as sharing or dependency: After the first stitch is worked, all the following stitches share at least one bead with another stitch. CRAW is a three-dimensional stitch. Before continuing with the instructions, please read the notes to the right for helpful information about the CRAW stitch.

## MATERIALS

- **16** 1.5mm Japanese seed beads (bead A)

- **28** 2mm Japanese seed beads (bead B)

- **32** 3mm Japanese seed beads (bead C)

- **24** 4mm fire-polished beads (bead D)

- pair of earring wires

- beading thread, diameter 00.20 (.008")

## TOOLS

- scissors

- big-eye needle

a

b

## MAKE THE EARRINGS

**NOTE:** *Create a tail long enough to wrap around your pinky finger. This will make it easier to hold onto your work. It also is easier to finish off a stitch when you know where it started.*

### MAKE CUBE 1

**1 | Make the base:** Thread a needle on 2½' of thread. Pick up 4D, leaving a 6" tail. Pass the needle through all four beads a second time and then through the first bead picked up **(photo a)**.

**2 | Make the wall/unit 1:** Pick up 3D. Pass through the bead your thread was exiting at the start of this step (starter bead) and through the next base bead **(photo b)**.

## Learning Made Easy

First a tip: If you can connect a new subject to something you already know, it is easier to learn. For example, CRAW is the beading equivalent to building a house of cards. The first card is the base of the house, and the first four beads stitched into a unit is the base of the stitch. The four cards that make up the walls share the base card for support. The four walls (the unit) of the stitch also share the base for support. In both cases, the walls are also dependent upon each other. The top card is the equivalent to the top four beads—they both become the base of another unit.

Second, I chose materials to clarify the stitch construction. Large beads make it easier to see the stitch, so I chose to start the stitch introduction with a 4mm bead. Using contrasting beads (color and sizes) provide visual clues to working the stitch.

**3 | Make the wall/unit 2:** Pick up 2D. Pass through the side bead from unit 1, the starter bead, and the next base bead **(photo c)**.

**4 | Make the wall/unit 3:** Pick up 2D. Pass through the side bead from unit 2, the starter bead, the fourth base bead, and the side bead of unit 1.

**5 | Make the wall/unit 4:** Only one bead is required to complete unit 4 because there are three beads available for sharing: the side bead from unit 3, the last available bead from the base, and one side bead from unit 1. Pick up 1D. Pass the needle down through the side bead of unit 3, through the last base bead, up through the side bead from unit 1, and through its top bead **(photo d)**.

**6 |** Pull the thread firmly so the four top beads are snug and pressed together. To strengthen the cube, pass through all four top beads two times. This will become the base for the next cube **(photo e)**.

**MAKE CUBE 2**
**7 | Make the wall/unit 1:** Pick up 3C. Pass through the starter bead and through the next bead of the base **(photo f)**.

**8 | Make the wall/unit 2:** Pick up 2C. Pass through the side bead from unit 1, the starter bead, and the next available base bead.

**9 | Make the wall/unit 3:** Pick up 2C. Pass through the side bead from unit 2, the starter bead, the last base bead, and the side bead from unit 1.

**10 | Make the wall/unit 4:** Pick up 1C. Pass the needle down through the side bead of unit 3, through the last base bead, up through the side bead from unit 1, and through its top bead **(photo g)**.

**11 |** Pull the thread firmly so the four top beads are snug and pressed together. To strengthen the cube, pass through all four top beads two times. This will become the base for the next cube.

**MAKE CUBE 3**
**12 |** Using Bs, repeat steps 7–11.

**MAKE CUBE 4**
**13 |** Using As, repeat steps 7–11.

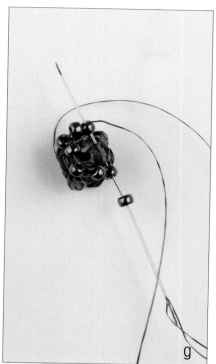

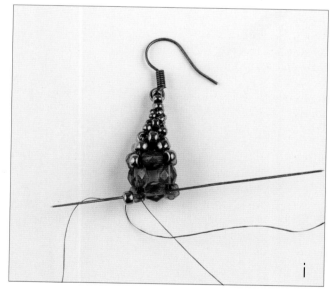

## ATTACH THE EARRING WIRE

**14 |** Pick up 3B, an earring wire, and 3B. Pass into the bead on the opposite corner and weave back to the starter bead. Retrace the path until secure **(photo h)**.

## EMBELLISH CUBE 1 WITH 8C

**NOTE:** *Make sure to follow the original stitch path whenever weaving through the beads or embellishing.*

**15 |** Weave your thread so it is exiting one of the Ds on the top of cube 1. **Side 1:** Fill in the four corners of one side of the first cube worked in D. Pick up 1C and pass through the next top D. Pick up 1C and pass down through the side D. Pick up 1C and pass through the bottom D **(photo i)**. Pick up 1C and pass up through the side D. In order to work the next side, you will have to step up by passing through the top three beads from side 1 (the first C added, the top D, and the second C added) and the top D from the next side to be embellished. **Side 2:** Pick up 1C and pass down through the D below. To complete this side, pick up 1C and pass through the next bead (the bottom D). Step up by passing through the beads shared with the first side (C, D, and C), the top D, the first C added to this side, and the top D from the next side. Repeat on side 3. If needed, reinforce the stitches by passing through the beads again, following the same thread path. Weave in the thread ends and trim.

**16 |** Make a second earring.

# Industrial Sunflower Pendant

While learning CRAW, you were introduced to the concept of bead sharing between stitches. In this project, you will take the concept of bead sharing to the next level by connecting two completed stitches (the first and the last) to complete the base form.

**NOTE:** *Wrapping the tail around your pinky finger will make it easier to hold onto your work. It also makes it easier to finish off a stitch because you'll know where it started.*

## PENDANT BASE

### MAKE THE FIRST STITCH

**1 | Make the base:** Thread a needle on 4' of thread. Pick up 4A, leaving a 12" tail. (Use the tail to attach the focal bead and top embellishments.) Pass through all four beads a second time and then through the first bead picked up.

**2 | Make wall/unit 1:** Pick up 3A. Pass through the bead your thread was exiting at the start of this step (starter bead) and through the next base bead.

**3 | Make wall/unit 2:** Pick up 2A. Pass through the side bead from unit 1, the starter bead, and the next base bead.

**4 | Make wall/unit 3:** Pick up 2A. Pass through the side bead from unit 2, the starter bead, the fourth base bead, and the side bead of unit 1.

**5 | Make wall/unit 4:** Only one bead is required to complete unit 4 because there are three beads available for sharing: the side bead from unit 3, the last available bead from the base, and one side bead from unit 1. Pick up 1A. Pass the needle down though the side bead of unit 3, through the last base bead, and up through the side bead from unit 1 and through its top bead.

**6 | Complete the stitch:** Pull the thread firmly so the four top beads are snug and pressed together. To strengthen the cube, pass through all four top beads twice. This will become the base for the next cube.

**7 |** Continue working in CRAW. Repeat steps 2–6 until you have worked a total of 11 cubes.

### CONNECT THE ENDS TO COMPLETE THE BASE

**NOTE:** *The twelfth stitch unit will be created when you join the ends together to create the base form. The four top beads from the eleventh cube will act as the base beads and the four bottom beads from the first cube will act as the top beads. (Make sure the piece is not twisted when connecting ends.)*

## MATERIALS

- 2g 11º Czech seed beads (bead A)

- **7** 3mm Japanese seed beads (bead B)

- **12** 1.5mm Japanese seed beads (bead C)

- **1** 6mm round fire-polished bead (bead D)

- **6** 6mm two-hole Chexx beads (bead E)

- **6** 6x12mm twisted daggers (bead F)

- **5** 4mm fire-polished beads (bead G)

- beading thread, diameter 00.20 (.008")

## TOOLS

- scissors

- **1** or **2** big-eye needles

- collapsible eye needle (optional)

**8 | Cube 12, make side 1:** This side is inside the circle. Pick up 1A, pass through the corresponding bead from the first cube, and pick up 1A. Complete the circuit by passing through the starter bead **(photo a)**. Pass through the first A picked up and the next available A from cube 1.

**9 | Make side 2:** Pick up 1A, and pass through the corresponding bead from cube 11, the A added for the previous side, and back through the starter bead **(photo b)**. Prepare for side 3 by weaving through the A added in this step and the next available A from cube 11.

**10 | Make side 3:** Pick up 1A. Pass through the corresponding bead from cube 1, the side bead from the previous step, and back through the starter bead. Prepare for side 4 by weaving through the A added in this step and the next available A on the fourth side.

**11 | Make side 4:** No beads are picked up. All the beads required for the fourth side are already there: 1A from cube 1, 1A from cube 11, 1A from side 1, and 1A from side 3. Pass through all four beads to create the fourth side **(photo c)**.

**EMBELLISH THE BASE**

**NOTE:** *You will embellish the outside edge first.*

**12 |** Attach a new thread so you have a second thread to add the top and bottom embellishment. Weave through the beadwork so one needle exits through a top edge bead and one needle exits through a bottom edge bead (they should be parallel to each other).

**13 | Embellish the bottom outside edge:** Pick up 1E, pass through the next A, pick up 1F, and pass through the next A. Repeat all the way around. Reinforce by passing through all the beads again. Step up by passing through the second hole of the first E picked up.

**14 | Create the bottom of the pendant base:** Pick up 3A and pass through the next E. Repeat all the way around **(photo d)**. Pass through all the beads (the As added and the Es passed through) a couple of times to create a secure bottom for the pendant.

**15 | Embellish the top outside edge:** Pick up 1B, pass through the next A, pick up 1B, pass through the next A, pick up 1G, and pass through the next A **(photo e)**. Repeat the process using the following bead pattern: 1B, 1G, 1B, 1G, 1B, 1G, 1B, 1G, 1B. Weave the thread so it is exiting an A under the center B of three B group.

**16 | Add the focal bead:** Pick up 1D. Pass through the bead opposite the starter bead, back through the bead picked up, and back through the starter bead. Finish the frame by working 1C into each A. Pick up 1C and pass through the next A. Repeat all the way around to add a total of 12C.

**17 | Create the bail:** The thread should be exiting the second hole of the first E picked up. Pick up 15A, pass through the center B, pick up 15A, and pass through the E again **(photo f)**. Retrace the thread path until secure. Weave the thread ends in and trim.

# Two-Strand CRAW Bracelet

## MATERIALS

*The bracelet is 7½", including the clasp.*

- 14g 2mm Japanese seed beads (bead A)

- **14** 4mm fire-polished beads (bead B)

- **10** 4mm fire-polished beads (bead C)

- **11** 4mm fire-polished beads (bead D)

- **2** 8x6mm end caps with loops

- **2** 5mm jump rings

- toggle clasp

- Beacon's Dazzle Tac

- beading thread, diameter 00.20 (.008")

## TOOLS

- scissors

- chainnose pliers

- bentnose pliers

- big-eye beading needle

This project allows you to apply what you learned from the previous pieces. It is a good idea to read through the entire project before starting. After writing up the instructions, I tried to put myself in the reader's position. Notes on materials, instructions, and constructions were added to answer the questions I thought you might have and to provide insight into decisions I made while developing this project.

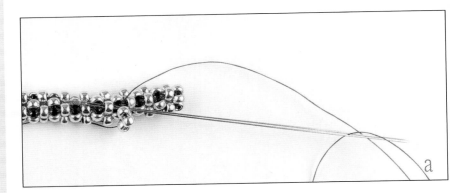

### STRAND 1

**1 | Make the base:** Thread a needle on 3' of thread. Pick up 4A, leaving a 6" tail. Pass through all four beads a second time, and then through the first bead picked up.

**2 | Make unit 1:** Pick up 3A. Pass through the starter bead and the next base bead.

**3 | Make unit 2:** Pick up 2A. Pass through the side bead from unit 1, the starter bead, and the next base bead.

**4 | Make unit 3:** Pick up 2A. Pass through the side bead from unit 2, the starter bead, the last base bead and the side bead from unit 1.

**5 | Make unit 4:** Pick up 1A. Pass down through the side bead of unit 3, the last base bead, the side bead from unit 1, and its top bead. Pull the thread firmly so the four top beads are snug and pressed together. To strengthen the cube, pass through all four top beads twice.

**6 |** To complete a strand, repeat steps 2–5 until there are a total of 43 cube units.

### STRAND 2

**7 |** Attach a new thread off of the fourth cube of strand 1. Treat a four-bead unit as the base unit for the second strand. **Make unit 1:** Pick up 3A. Pass through the starter bead and the next base bead **(photo a)**.

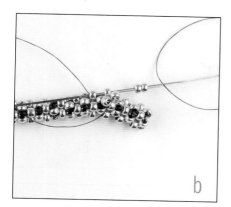

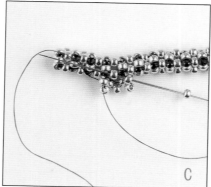

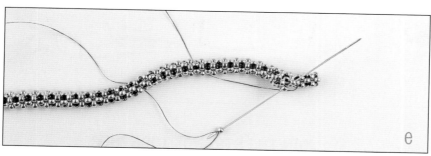

**8 | Make unit 2:** Pick up 2A. Pass through the side bead from unit 1, the starter bead, and the next base bead **(photo b)**. **Make unit 3:** Pick up 2A. Pass through the side bead from unit 2, the starter bead, the last base bead, and the side bead from unit 1. **Make unit 4:** Pick up 1A. Pass down through the side bead of unit 3, the last base bead, the side bead from unit 1, and its top bead **(photo c)**. Pull the thread firmly, bringing the four top beads together. Pass through the four top beads two times.

### CREATE A STRAND TRANSITION

**NOTE:** *To create the look of a more gradual addition of a second strand, you'll work a modified stitch below the first stitch you just added and off the side of the third cube from strand number one. (The four beads that make up the side of cube 3 will become the base of the transition unit.) Weave the thread so it is exiting a side bead from the third stitch unit.*

**9 |** Pick up 1A, pass through 1A above from the first cube of the second strand and down through the starter bead. (You added 1A and worked a 3A stitch.) Weave the needle to the next bead **(photo d)**.

**10 |** Pick up 1A. Pass through the following; the 1A from the stitch above, the 1A from the prior stitch, the starter base bead and the bead just added. (You added 1A and worked a 4A stitch.) **(photo e)**.

**11 |** The method for finishing the strand connector is like the very last step to finish off the cube. You aren't adding new beads; you are creating a secure connection

amongst the beads. I used pins to identify the 4A **(photo f)**. Pass through the 4A to create a closed unit. Then weave the needle so it is exiting a top bead from the first cube created for strand 2.

**12 |** Continue to work in CRAW until the second strand has 39 cube units.

### MAKE THE CENTER EMBELLISHMENT

**13 |** Thread a needle on 4' of thread, and pick up 4A, leaving a 12" tail. Pass through all four beads again and the first three beads.

**14 |** Pick up 1B, 1C, and 1D. Pass through the bead the thread was exiting at the start of this step (starter bead) and the first two beads picked up.

**15 |** Pick up 1A, 1B, 1A, 1D, and 1A. Pass through the starter bead and the first three beads picked up.

**16 |** Pick up 3A. Pass through the starter bead and the first two beads picked up.

**17 |** Pick up 1C, 1D, and 1B. Pass through the starter bead and the first two beads picked up.

**18 |** Pick up 1A, 1C, 1A, 1B, and 1A. Pass through the starter bead and the first three beads picked up.

**19 |** Pick up 3A. Pass through the starter bead and the first two beads picked up.

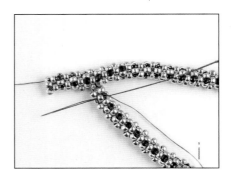

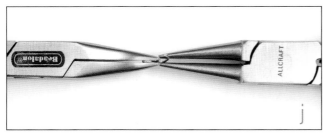

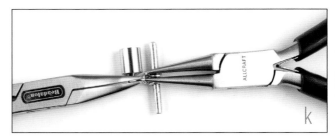

**20 |** Repeat steps 14–19 two more more times.

**21 |** Pick up 1B, 1C, and 1D. Pass through the starter bead and the first two beads picked up.

**21 |** Pick up 1A, 1B, 1A, 1D, and 1A. Pass through the starter bead and the first three beads picked up.

**22 |** Pick up 3A. Pass through the starter bead and the first two beads picked up.

## ATTACH THE CENTER EMBELLISHMENT

**NOTE:** *There is a four-bead unit at both ends of the center embellishment. The connection to the strands will be made from the side beads of the four-bead unit. There will be a total of four connection points, two at each end. The first connection point is the seventh cube unit of strand 1.*

**23 |** Both ends of the embellishment have a 4A unit. The thread should be exiting from one of those 4A units. Pick up 3A. Pass through the starter bead and the first 2A beads picked up.

**24 |** Pick up 1A. Pass through a side bead from the third unit from where the two strands joined together. Pick up 1A. Pass through the starter bead and the other 3A that make up the 4A unit a couple of times until secure. Weave thread to the other side unit and repeat the attachment process **(photo g)**.

**25 |** Repeat steps 23 and 24 to attach the other end.

## JOIN THE STRANDS TOGETHER

**26 |** You will join the second strand at the 40th unit of strand 1. The thread should be exiting an end bead from strand 2. Pick up 1A, pass through a side 1A from strand 1, and pick up 1A **(photo h)**. Pass through the starter bead (to complete the circuit) and the next bead. With the next two sides, only pick up 1A to complete a four-bead unit **(photo i)**. For the last side, zero beads are picked up. Pass through the existing 4A.

**27 |** Apply the strand transition after the two strands are joined together. Repeat steps 9–11 (do not weave the needle so it is exiting a top bead from the first cube created for strand 2 because the strand is complete).

## ATTACH THE CLASP

**28 | Connect the bead caps to the clasp:** Use pliers to open a jump ring. The movement to open it is like arm wrestling. Imagine that each plier holding the jump ring is like an arm wrestler trying to push their side of the opening towards their opponent **(photo j)**. Slip the bead cap and half of the clasp onto the jump ring, and close. Repeat on the other end of the bracelet **(photo k)**.

**29 |** Glue the bead caps onto the ends of the bracelet. Make sure to follow manufacturer's instructions.

**TIP:** *Glue can come out of the tube quickly. The cleanest way to apply glue is to first squeeze it out onto wax paper or a paper plate and then dip the end of the bracelet into the glue.*

# Modern Romance Ring

The herringbone stitch is also known as Ndebele stitch. Unlike other stitches, you will pick up two beads at a time. In this project, you will learn how to work the easiest version of the stitch by making a ring with a band that is one stitch wide. You could also think of the band as having one stitch per row.

## MATERIALS

- **4** 1.5mm Japanese seed beads (bead A)

- 2g 2mm Japanese seed beads (bead B)

- **4** 3mm Japanese seed beads (bead C)

- **1** 5mm cubic zirconia round bead (bead D)

- **2** two-hole Brick beads (bead E)

- beading thread, diameter 00.20 (.008")

## TOOLS

- scissors

- big-eye needle

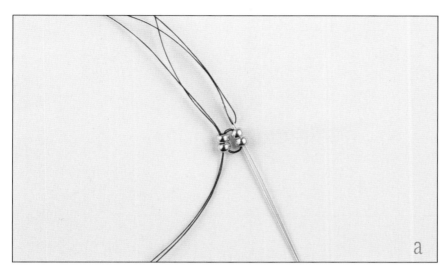

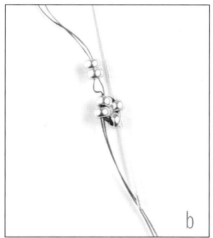

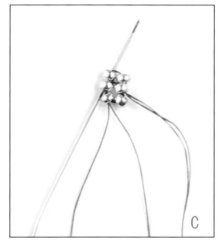

## MAKE THE RING

**1 | Create a ladder stitch base:** Thread a needle on 6' of thread doubled over. Pick up 4B, leaving a 4" tail. Pass through all four beads again to create a two-by-two square, and then pass back up through the bottom of the first two beads picked up **(photo a)**.

**2 | Work in herringbone stitch:** Pick up 2B. Pass down through the next bead and back up through the starter bead (the bead the thread was exiting at the start of the step) and the first bead picked up **(photos b and c)**. Work another 10 stitches in this manner.

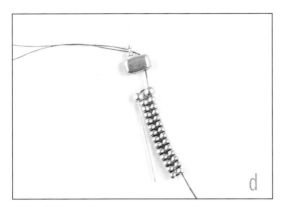

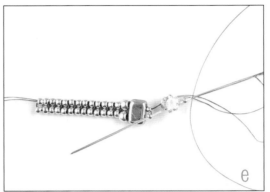

**3** | Work one stitch using Cs.

**4** | Pick up 1E and 2A. Pass down through the second hole of the E and the C below, and then go up through the next bead, the E, and the first A picked up **(photo d)**.

**5** | **Add the focal bead:** Pick up 1D and 2A. Pass down through the second hole of the D and the A below and back up through the starter bead, the D, and the first A picked up **(photo e)**.

**6** | Pick up 1E and 2C. Pass down through the second hole of the E and the A below it. Then pass back up through the starter bead, the E, and the first C picked up.

**7** | Using Bs, continue working in herringbone stitch until the band wraps around your finger.

**8** | Connect the two ends of the band by following the same bead path as the herringbone stitch without adding any additional beads. Treat the two beads at the beginning of the band as if you were adding them. Pass into the closest bead and back out through the second bead. To complete the circuit, pass into the last bead added and the starter bead **(photo f)**. Reinforce by repeating the path. Weave the thread ends in and trim.

# Traditional Triple-Strand Bracelet

## Practice

## MATERIALS

*The bracelet is 6½" long, including the clasp.*

- **1** hank 10º Czech seed beads (bead A)

- **30** Tila beads (bead B)

- **13** two-hole Brick beads (bead C)

- **12** 4x6mm Pellet beads (bead D)

- 16x10mm two-strand slide-lock clasp

- beading thread, diameter 0.20 (.008")

## TOOLS

- scissors

- big-eye needle

In this second herringbone project, you will practice what you learned from the first: working the herringbone stitch in a strand that is one stitch wide. Unlike the band in the first project, the bracelet end brackets have rows of multiple stitches. This means you will learn how to transition from one stitch to the next. Plus, you'll learn to modify the stitch in order to use a variety of beads (seed beads, two-hole Tila beads, two-hole Brick beads, and Pellet beads).

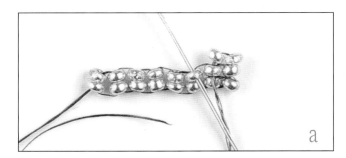

a

## THREAD LENGTH

The thread lengths given are suggestions. For the first bracket, I used 6' of thread and centered the first two beads picked up. The 3' below the first two beads picked up (the tail) will be used to work the third strand and the working thread will be used to work the first strand. This reduces the number of times thread has to be added. I used 2' of thread on the second bracket, with a tail of about 8".

To avoid confusion, you can weave the tail end through the beads so it is exiting the opposite side of the working thread.

## CREATE TWO END BRACKETS

**1 |** Thread a needle on 6' of thread (see note above). **Create an eight-bead ladder stitch base:** Pick up 4A. Pass up through the first 2A and down through the last 2A, creating two columns of 2A. You will pick up 2A for the subsequent stitches. Pick up 2A. Pass through previous 2A and then through the added 2A. Continue working in ladder stitch, to make a ladder that is eight beads long. Weave the thread around so it is exiting from the last bead on the top. After the eighth stitch (column), pass up through the second-to-last bead on the bottom row and the last bead on the top row.

**2 | Start working in herringbone stitch:** Pick up 2A. Pass down through the second bead and up through the third bead **(photo a)**. Repeat to the end of the row. After the last stitch, weave the thread around so the thread is exiting the last bead on the third row.

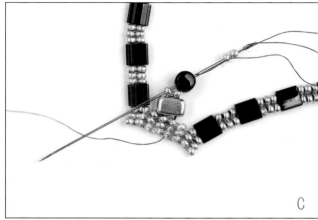

## CREATE STRANDS

**3 | Create the first and third strand using the same bead pattern:** Work the first strand off the first two 2A and the third off of the last 2A. Pick up 1B. Pass down through the second hole of the Tila bead and the second A directly below it **(photo b)**. Pass up through the first A and the first hole of the B. Pick up 2A. Pass down through the second hole of the B. Pass up through the first hole of the B and the first A picked up. Work two more stitches using A. Continue the pattern until you have added 15A to the strand or until you have achieved the desired length. Flip the piece over so the last two beads become the first two beads.

**4 | Create the center strand:** It is worked off the center two seed beads (which means using one bead from two different stitches), leaving one seed bead space before and after the center column. Attach a new piece of thread that is 3' long, leaving an 8" tail. Pick up 1C. Pass down through the second hole of the C and the seed bead directly below. Pass up through the next seed bead and the first hole of the C. Pick up 2A. Pass down through the second hole of the C. Pass up through the first hole of the brick bead and the first A picked up. *Here's a stitch modification:* Pick up 1D and 2A. Pass down through the D and the second A below **(photo c)**. Pass up through the first A below the D, the D, and the first A picked up. Repeat the pattern until you have added 13C or until you reach the desired length. The last bead added should be just a single C.

**NOTE:** *The center strand is slightly longer than the other two.*

## ATTACH THE END BRACKET AND CLASP

**5 | Attach each strand to the second bracket:** Follow the thread path as though you are working a herringbone stitch **(photo d)**. Secure the strand by retracing the thread path for a few stitches.

**6 | Attach the clasp**: The clasp is sewn to the center two stitches at each end and the thread path is similar to that of the herringbone stitch. Weave the thread so it is exiting one of these stitches. Pass through the clasp loop, through the second bead of that stitch, and up through the first bead of the stitch **(photo e)**. Retrace the path until secure. Use the same method to attach the second clasp loop. Weave in the thread ends and trim. Repeat on the other end of the bracelet.

**NOTE:** *In the base row of the herringbone stitch, all the beads are connected at the top and bottom. (Please refer to* **photo a**.) *To make the inside edge neater, connect the top row of beads.*

# Radiant Sundial Bracelet

While making this project, you get to apply what you learned about the herringbone stitch, such as working with a two-bead stitch, transitioning from stitch to stitch, and transitioning from row to row. As a reader bonus, I included an alternate version of the bracelet made using the tubular herringbone stitch. (To me, transitioning from row to row in tubular herringbone is easier than with flat herringbone.)

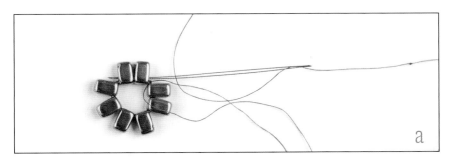

## MATERIALS

*The bracelet is 7" long, including the clasp.*

- **1** hank 11º Czech seed beads (bead A)
- **8** 11º Czech seed beads (bead B)
- 7g 2mm Japanese seed beads (bead C)
- 7g 3mm Japanese seed beads (bead D)
- **8** two-hole Brick beads (bead E)
- **1** 8mm fire-polished bead (bead F)
- **10** 4mm fire-polished beads (bead G) (flat herringbone band) OR **18** 4mm fire-polished beads (tubular herringbone band)
- toggle clasp
- **2** 7mm ribbon ends (flat herringbone band) OR **2** 8x6mm end caps with loops (tubular herringbone band; see tip on p. 60)
- **2** 5mm jump rings
- Beacon's Dazzle Tac
- beading thread, diameter 00.20 (.008")

## TOOLS
- scissors
- big-eye needle
- chainnose pliers
- bentnose pliers

## MAKE THE BRACELET
**NOTE:** *The Brick bead is a two-hole bead. The hole originally passed through to pick up the beads will be referred to as the inside hole. The second hole will be referred to as the outside hole.*

### FOCAL COMPONENT
**1 |** Thread a needle on an 18" piece of thread. Pick up 8E, leaving a 4" tail. Pass through the same hole in all the beads again and tie into a knot with the working thread and tail **(photo a)**.

**2 | Pick up and attach the focal bead:** Pick up 1F. Pass through the inside hole of an E on the opposite side **(photo b)**. Secure the bead by passing through half of the Es on the left and the bead picked up. Then repeat on the right.

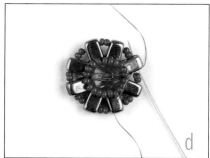

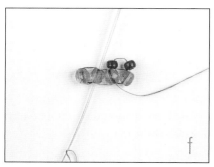

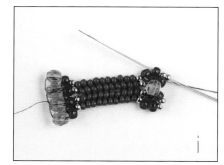

**3 | Frame the focal bead:** Pick up 10A. Pass through F **(photo c)**. Repeat on the other side.

**4 | Secure the focal bead frame:** Weave back and forth from Brick bead to seed beads. Pass the needle through a few seed beads and then through the inside hole of the closest E. Repeat all the way around. Tighten the frame by passing through all the framing beads. Reinforce as needed to make the component firm. Weave the thread ends in and trim.

**5 |** Thread a needle on a new 2' piece of thread. Pass through the outside hole of an E, leaving an 8" tail. Pick up 2A. Pass through the outside hole of the next E **(photo d)**. Repeat all the way around. Step up by passing through the first A picked up in this step.

**6 |** Pick up 1B. Pass through the next A, E, and A **(photo e)**. Repeat all the way around. After the eighth B has been added, step up by weaving your thread through the beads until it is exiting the A following the first B added in this step.

**MAKE TWO FLAT HERRINGBONE BANDS**
**7 | Create a four-bead ladder strip base:**
Thread a needle on 4' of thread. Pick up 2G, leaving a 10" tail, and pass up through the bottom of the first bead and down through the top of the second. Pick up 1G. Pass through the previous bead and the bead just picked up. Repeat to add the fourth bead. Work with tight tension so the beads sit neatly together. Reinforce by zig-

zagging through the beads. Exit the top of the first bead picked up, opposite the tail.

**8 | Start working in the herringbone stitch:**
Pick up 2D, pass down through the second G, and go up through the third G **(photo f)**. Pick up 2D and pass down through the next G. Weave the thread around so it is exiting the last D added.

**9 |** Continue working the band in the flat herringbone stitch as follows: one row of C, 10 rows of A, one row of C, and one row of D. After you have completed the D row, weave the thread so it is exiting a center D.

**10 | Add 1G to the center of the band:** Pick up 1G and pass the needle down through the other center D **(photo g)**. Pass up through the closest D at the end. Work the first herringbone stitch using D **(photo h)**. Pass through the G and up through the next D. Work the second herringbone stitch using Ds. The next row is worked using Cs.

**NOTE:** *Pull the thread tight between stiches to close the space between them and this will push the G to the top* **(photo i)**.

**11 | Continue working in herringbone stitch to complete the band:** Using As, work another 12 rows or until you reach the desired length. Repeat to make another band.

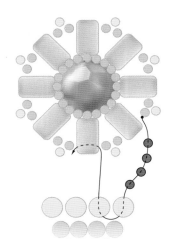

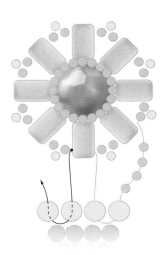

figure 1

figure 2

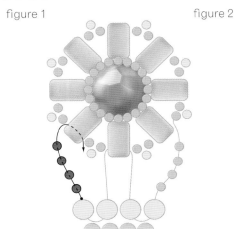

figure 3

## ATTACH THE FOCAL COMPONENT

**12 |** Your thread should be exiting the A just before the E. Pick up 4A and pass into the band through a G. Pass out through the next G on the left. Connect to the focal component by passing through E from the right side **(figure 1)**. Pass into the band again through the next G and out through the next G **(figure 2)**. Pick up 4A. The next time the needle passes through the focal component, it should mirror the first connection between the two pieces. The needle should pass through the third E (entering from the left side) **(figure 3)**. Retrace the thread path to secure. Repeat this process to attach the second band. Weave in the thread ends and trim.

## ATTACH THE CLASP

**13 | Connect the clasp to the ribbon ends using jump rings:** Use pliers to open the jump rings. Slip a ribbon end and one half of the clasp onto the jump ring, and close the jump ring **(photo j)**. Repeat on the other end of the bracelet.

**14 |** Follow the manufacturer's instructions for gluing. Glue and squeeze the ribbon ends into place **(photo k)**. Let dry.

# MAKE TWO TUBULAR HERRINGBONE BANDS (ALTERNATE VERSION)

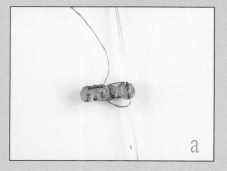

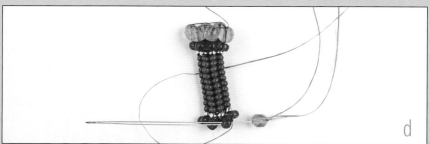

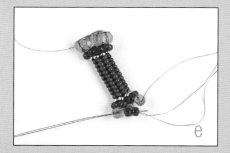

**1 |** Make a focal component following steps 1–6, p. 57.

**2 | Create a six-bead ladder stitch ring:**
Thread a needle on 5' of thread and pick up 2G, leaving a 10" tail. Pass the needle up through the bottom of the first bead and down through the second bead picked up. Pick up 1G. Pass through the previous G and the G just picked up. Repeat three more times. Form a ring by passing through the first G picked up, down through the last G, and back up through the first G **(photo a)**. (The working thread is exiting the top of the first bead picked up opposite the tail.) Pull tight to create a secure ring.

**3 | Start working in the tubular herringbone stitch:** Pick up 2D, and pass down through the second G and up through the next G **(photo b)**. Repeat. **Work the third and last stitch in the row:** Pick up 2D and pass down through the next G. The last stitch in tubular herringbone differs from the last stitch of flat herringbone, as you pass up through two beads: the bead the thread was exiting at the start of the row and the first bead picked up **(photo c)**.

**4 |** Continue working the band in tubular herringbone stitch as follows: one row of C, 10 rows of A, one row of C, and one row of D.

**5 | Work 1G into each stitch:** Pick up 1G, pass down through the next D, and go up through the third D **(photo d)**. Repeat two more times. **After the third stitch, complete the standard end-of-row**

**step up:** Pass up through the D your thread was exiting at the start of this row and the first G picked up.

**6 | Work 2D into each stitch:** Pick up 2D and pass through the next bead **(photo e)**. Repeat three times. After the third stitch, step up by passing through the first D picked up.

**7 |** Continue working in tubular herringbone to complete the band. Work one row using Cs. Using As, work another 12 rows or the number rows needed to achieve the desired size. Repeat to make another band.

**8 |** Attach the focal component to the band, following step 12, p. 59.

**9 |** Attach the end cap to the clasp, following step 13, p. 59.

**10 |** Apply the glue to the band according to the manufacturer's instructions, insert the band into the end cap, and let it dry.

**TIP:** *Wait until you have completed the band of the tubular herringbone version before buying the end caps. This way you will be certain that they will fit. The end caps might not fit if the seed beads are a slightly different size (see Basics). Your tension or the tightness of how you work the stitch might vary, and the end cap dimension could be off as well.*

# Square Stitch

Grandmother's Cocktail Ring

Each bead worked in square stitch sits squarely on top of the bead in the row below it. The square stitch lends itself to geometric patterns or to any design that you want to be neat and tidy. This ring is reminiscent of the cocktail rings my grandmother used to wear. Traditionally, a cocktail ring is meant to be a dramatic, large ring worn at a cocktail party. Today, people wear cocktail rings whenever they want to add some pop to their style.

## MATERIALS
- 2g 11º Japanese seed beads (bead A)
- **1** 8mm fire-polished bead (bead B)
- beading thread, diameter 00.20 (.008")

## TOOLS
- scissors
- **2** big-eye needles

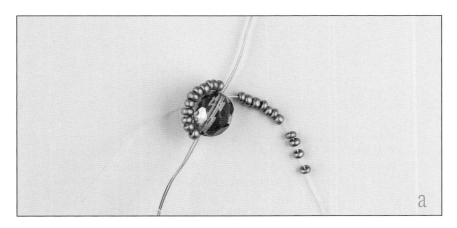

a

b

## MAKE THE RING
**NOTES:** *Fitting a ring is easier to do when you work both band sides simultaneously and have them meet on the palm side of the hand.*

**1 |** Thread a needle with 4' of thread. Pick up 1B and 11A, leaving a 2' tail. Pass through all the beads two more times. Attach the second needle to the tail. Pick up 11A. Pass through the B and the beads just picked up two times **(photo a)**.

**2 | Start the band on either side of the focal component:** Pick up 1A. Pass through the bead directly below and through the bead that was just picked up **(photo b)**. The new bead sits on top of the old bead and the holes are horizontal. Work a total of 11 stitches.

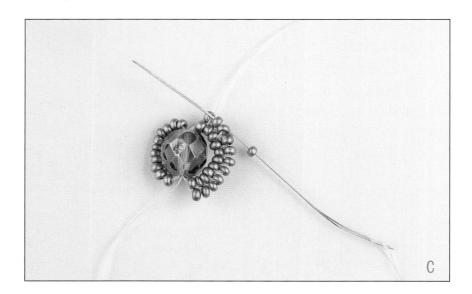

After the last stitch, weave the thread around so that the needle is exiting the second-to-last stitch of the row you just completed **(photo c)**.

**NOTE:** *Steps 3–5 apply to both sides of the band. Three stitch rows are worked until you achieve the desired size and the ends meet in the middle.*

**3 |** Work nine square stitches. Again, after the last stitch, weave the thread around so the needle is exiting the second-to-last bead from the end.

**4 |** Continue working in this manner until you have a three-bead unit.

**5 |** Continue working three-bead rows until you reach the desired size. Finish off one side of the band by weaving the thread end in and trim.

**6 | Connect the two side of the band together:** The beads on the finished side are treated as though you were adding them to the side with the working thread. Pass through the closest A on the finished side, the A the needle was originally exiting, and the A on the finished end again. Repeat two more times. Weave the thread end in and trim.

# Vintage-Inspired Dragonfly Pin

## MATERIALS

- 2g 1.5mm Japanese seed beads (bead A)

- **20** 2mm Japanese seed beads (bead B)

- **9** 3mm Japanese seed beads (bead C)

- **12** 6º Japanese seed beads (bead D)

- **14** 4mm fire-polished beads (bead E)

- beading thread, diameter 00.20 (.008")

## TOOLS

- scissors

- big-eye needle

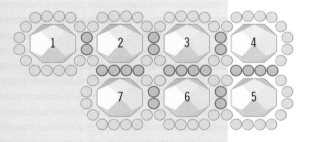

figure 1

The neatness of the square stitch lends itself well to this project. The stitch is used to create a setting for the beads that make up the wings. After creating the setting for the first bead of a wing, the construction of the setting for additional framed beads borrows from the construction of the right-angle weave stitch. When units are added, beads are shared with the prior unit.

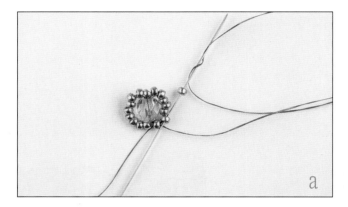

### MAKE TWO WINGS

**NOTE:** *Each side of the 4mm bead will be framed with eight beads for a total of 16. After the first 4mm bead unit, each following unit will share beads with the previous unit.*

#### ROW 1

**1 |** Thread a needle on 4' of thread, leaving an 8" tail. **Make unit 1:** Pick up 1E and 8A. Pass through E. Pick up 8A and pass through the center E. Pass through all As picked up (consider this the bottom row). Pick up 1A. Pass through the A directly below and through the bead that was just picked up **(photo a)**. Work a total of 16 square stitches. Connect the ends by passing through four As: the 2A that make up the first stitch and 2A that make up the last stitch **(photo b)**. Repeat the path through all four As until secure. Pass through the middle of E and between rows 1 and 2 of the bead frame.

**2 | Make unit 2:** Pick up 1E and 7A. Pass through one of the A from the bottom row that is being shared with the prior unit and E. (The shared beads are shown in red in **figure 1**.) Pick up 7A. Pass through the shared 2A shared (bottom row). Pass through the top row of the two shared stitches **(photo c)**. Work 14A in the square stitch. Close the frame by passing through the top row of the first shared bead **(photo d)**. Prepare for the next unit by weaving around so you can pass through E and exit between the top and bottom row. (It is best to wait until the end to tighten up the beads that frame the Es.)

**3 | Make units 3 and 4:** Work as in unit 2.

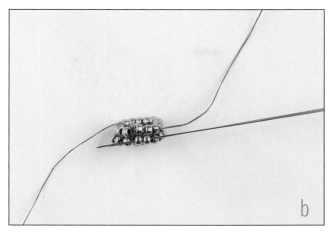

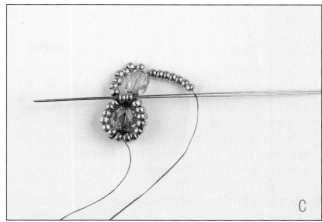

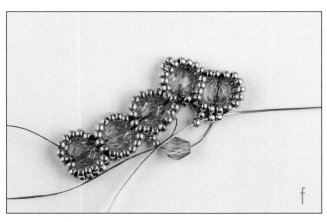

## ROW 2

**NOTE:** *Each unit will share four beads with the unit above it from row one. Units 4 and 5 will connect to the body.*

**4 | Make unit 5:** The needle should be exiting the bead shown in green in the chart. Pick up 2A, 1E, and 2A. Pass the needle through the four shared beads shown in red in **figure 1** and the first 2A picked up **(photo e)**. Pick up 8A and pass through the center E. Using As, work the square stitch in the first 2A picked up. Pass through the top row of the four stitches shared with the previous unit. Work 10A in square stitch. Close the frame by connecting the first and last stitches together. Prepare for the next unit by passing through E and exiting between the rows of seed beads.

**5 | Make unit 6 (shares beads with two units):** Pick up 1E and 2A, and pass through the four beads it shares with unit from row 1. Pick up 1A and pass through the 2A it shares with the unit prior **(photo f)**. Pick up 7A, pass through the center E and the top row of the two stitch it shares with the previous unit. Work 9A in square stitch. Pass through the top row of the shared 4A. Work 1A in square stitch. Pass through the top row of the 2A shared and the 7A added. Prepare for the next

unit by by weaving around and passing through E and exiting between the rows of seed beads.

**6 | Make unit 7:** Repeat step 5.

## MAKE THE HEAD

**NOTE:** *See* **figure 2**, *p. 68, to construct the head and body of the dragonfly.*

**7 |** Thread a needle on 2' of thread. Pick up 1C, 3D, and 1C.

**8 |** Pick up 1C, and pass through the last C picked up from step 1 and through the bead that was just picked up. Continue working in square stitch, following the established bead pattern. Weave the thread around so the needle is exiting a D from the second-to-last stitch.

**9 | Create the top of the head:** The bead pattern for this row is 1C, 1D, and 1C. Pick up one bead at a time. Pass through the stitch below and the bead just picked up. Weave the thread to the center D at the bottom.

## MAKE THE BODY

**10 |** The body is made up of 5D and 3C. Beads are added one at a time and worked in the ladder stitch. Pick up 1D. Pass through the prior bead and the bead added. Continue with the remaining Cs. Work the thread back up to the 4th D added for the body.

**11 |** Pick up 3B and pass through the D above. Pick up 3B and pass through the D below and the first 3B added. Repeat three times. Pick up 1B and pass through the center bead of the base of the head. Pick up 1B and pass through the bead below. Then pass through all the Bs added in this step. The thread should be exiting the fourth D from the base of the head.

## ASSEMBLE THE PIN

**12 | Attach the wings:** The wings are attached to the Bs along the sides of the body. Line up the bottom of the wings with the Bs. Sew through the beads as if you were working in square stitch. Tighten the tension, if needed, when you weave the threads in and trim.

**13 | Attach the pin finding:** Sew through the D to attach the pin back. Weave in the ends and trim.

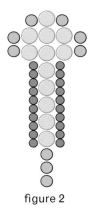

figure 2

# Design Inspiration

When I think of vintage costume jewelry, I think of jewelry created by artisans of the top jewelry houses when they moonlighted to make ends meet during the Great Depression. The craftsmanship of their work inspired my love of vintage costume jewelry and this dragonfly pin.

# Ethnic Spice Bracelet

## Apply

This project gives you the opportunity to apply what you have learned about the square stitch. The name of the stitch is square, but this project has lots of curves.

## MATERIALS

*The bracelet is 7³/₄" long, including the clasp.*

- 2g 2mm Japanese seed beads, primary color (bead A)

- 3g 3mm Japanese seed beads, primary color (bead B)

- 1g 2mm Japanese seed beads, secondary color (bead C)

- **20** 3mm Japanese seed beads, secondary color (bead D)

- **10** 8mm fire-polished beads (bead E)

- toggle clasp

- beading thread, diameter 00.20 (.008")

## TOOLS

- scissors

- big-eye needle

**NOTE:** *Ten-link units are created for this bracelet. On the odd-numbered links, the secondary color beads are placed on the right side of the center bead. Switch to the left side on the even-numbered links.*

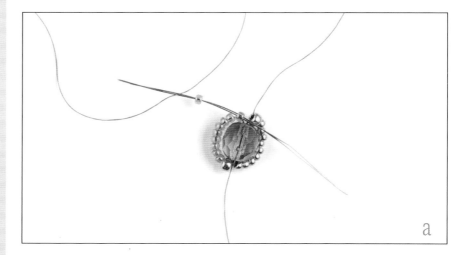

## LINK 1

**1 |** Thread a needle on a comfortable length of thread and pick up 1E, 1D, and 9C, leaving a 10" tail. Pass the needle through the center E, all of the seed beads, and the E again. (Place the seed beads to the right side of the center bead.)

**2 |** Pick up 9A and 1D. Pass through the center E and all of the seed beads picked up for this link.

**3 | Work the first row of square stitches over the As:** Pick up 1A. Pass through the A below and the bead just added **(photo a)**. Repeat for a total of nine stitches.

**4 |** Work a second row of square stitches using Bs.

**5 | Work two square stitches in the secondary color (the opposite side):** Pick up 1B and work as a square stitch into the D on the secondary color side. Pick up 1A and work as a square stitch into the first C picked up.

## LINK 2

**6|** Pick up 1E, 1D, and 9C. Pass through the center E, all the seed beads, and the E again. Make sure the new link sits snugly on top of the previous link. Remember, the secondary color is on the left side on even-numbered links.

**7 |** Pick up 9A and 1D. Pass up through the center E and down through all the seed beads added in this step.

**8 | Connect the two links:** Going in the same direction, pass through the first C picked up in the previous link and then, going in the opposite direction, pass through the A above it and the beads picked up in the previous step **(photos b and c)**.

**9 |** Work 9A in square stitch over the 9A.

**10 |** Work 9B in square stitch over the 9A.

**11 |** Work two square stitches into the left side. Pick up 1B and work as a square stitch into the D on the left side. Pick up 1A and work as a square stitch into the first C picked up.

**12 |** Continue adding links until you have 10 links or the desired length. The last link ends with the ninth B. Then weave your thread so that it is exiting the A bead below.

## FINISH THE PIECE

**13 | Create clasp connectors using Cs and working in square stitch:** The tail will be used to create a connector off of the first link worked. The thread should be exiting the closest C. Pick up 1C and work a square stitch into the C below **(photo d)**. Pick up 1C and work a square stitch in the D below. Continue working in square stitch. On the side the bar will be attached, work five rows in square stitch using Cs. On the side the ring will be attached, work three rows using Cs.

**14 | Attach the clasp:** Using a figure-8 thread path allows it to lay flat. Weave the thread so it is exiting between the pair of beads. Pass through the clasp and through the left bead. Repeat on the right **(photo e)**. Repeat on both sides until secure. Weave the thread in and trim.

# *Circular Brick Stitch*

# Circles in Time Earrings

The circular brick stitch is versatile because of the many ways you might begin. This stitch can be worked off of a round bead, another shaped bead, or even a metal ring! The circular brick stitch can be used to make pendants or charms, or it may be used as part of a larger beadweaving project.

## MATERIALS

- **45–60** 2mm Japanese seed beads (bead A)

- **30–40** 3mm Japanese seed beads (bead B)

- **40–50** 11º Czech seed beads (bead C)

- **2** 8mm glass coin beads (bead D)

- pair of earring wires

- beading thread, diameter 00.20 (.008")

## TOOLS

- scissors

- big-eye needle

- big-eye collapsible needle

**NOTE:** *It can be frustrating when the bead follows the needle under the loop and prevents you from finishing the stitch. Try this technique: After the needle is halfway under the bridge, rest your pointer finger of the hand holding the piece on top of the needle. This will help prevent the bead from going under the bridge and you'll be able to finish the stitch.*

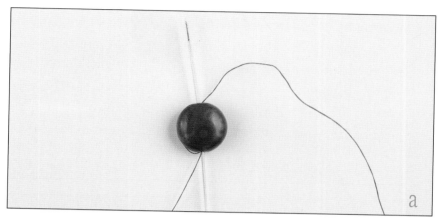

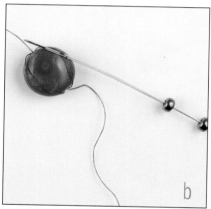

## MAKE THE EARRINGS

**1 |** Thread a needle on 2½' of thread and pick up the coin bead, leaving a 5" tail. Pass through the center twice, placing one loop of thread on each side of the bead. The stitches that surround the center coin bead will be worked off of these loops **(photo a)**.

**2 |** Every row of the brick stitch starts with two beads. The first row is done using the B. Pick up 2B **(photo b)**. Pass the needle under the thread loop (heading towards you) and up through second bead picked up **(photo c)**. Pull the thread so the beads rest snugly on the center bead. (You may need to use your fingers to nudge the beads into place.)

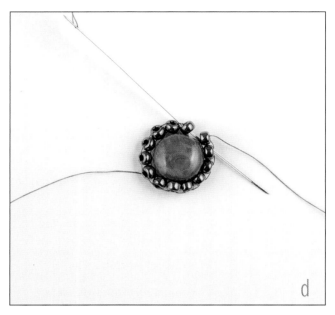

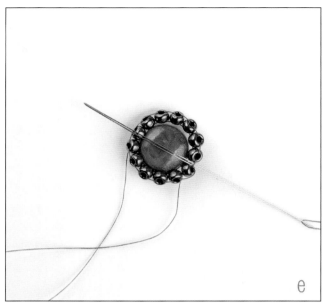

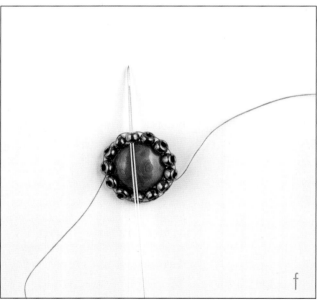

**3 | Finish the round, picking up one bead at a time:** Pick up 1B, pass under the loop, and then pass back up through the bead. Repeat all the way around the center bead until you have added a total of 13 beads. (The number may vary based on the bead you use. Make sure the Bs are evenly spaced around the center bead.) After you complete the last stitch, pass down through the first bead **(photo d)**, out towards the back, under the thread loop in front of the first bead **(photo e)**, and up through the first bead **(photo f)**.

**4 | Continue working in circular brick stitch:** Work 23C for round 2 and 25A for round 3.

**5 | Attach the earring wire:** Pick up 2B, an earring wire, and 2B. Pass down through the A next to the starting bead and back through the bead exited at the start of this step **(photo g)**. Repeat the thread path several times to secure. Weave the thread ends in and trim.

# Enchanting Butterfly Pin

**Practice**

## MATERIALS

- **1** hank 10° Czech seed beads (bead A)

- **11** 11° Japanese seed beads (bead B)

- **3** 8° Japanese seed beads (bead C)

- **4** 6mm pressed glass beads (bead D)

- **3** 3mm fire-polished beads (bead E)

- **5** 4mm fire-polished beads (bead F)

- **1** two-hole Brick bead (bead G)

- **4** 8mm closed rings (links)

- 20mm pin back

- beading thread, diameter 00.20 (.008")

## TOOLS

- scissors

- big-eye needle

- big-eye collapsible needle (optional)

As you may recall from the first circular brick project, this stitch can be worked off a ring. The following butterfly project was originally created to be an aesthetic reference of how the butterfly could look if it were worked off a round bead. I hope you enjoy the end result!

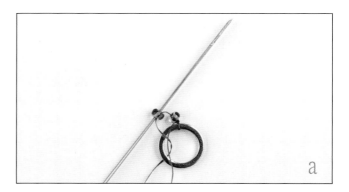

## MAKE THE BOTTOM HALF OF THE WING

**NOTE:** *Normally, circular brick stitch is flat like the earrings in the stitch introduction. To give the butterfly dimension and create design interest, I chose to use one less bead in the fourth row. If you prefer a flat butterfly, work an additional bead into that round.*

**1 |** Thread a needle on a 2' piece of thread, and tie a knot around the ring, leaving a 6" tail. Pick up 2A. Pass the needle under the frame (heading toward you) and up through the second bead picked up **(photo a)**. Pull the thread so the beads rest snugly on the center ring. (You may need to use your fingers to nudge the beads into place.) Pick up 1A, and pass the needle under the frame and back up through the third bead. Repeat all the way around the ring until you have worked a total of 13 As. (The number may vary based on the ring you use. Space the beads evenly around the ring.) After you complete the last stitch, pass down through the first bead, out towards the back, under the frame in front of the first bead, and through the first bead **(photo b)**.

**2 | Attach the flat, round bead using the thread tail:** Pass the thread tail through a needle. Pick up 1D. Pass through a bead on the opposite side **(photo c)**. The needle should exit the outside edge of the bead. The return path starts by passing through the next bead heading toward the center. Pass through the D again. Pass out through one bead and back in toward the center. Repeat a couple of times to secure.

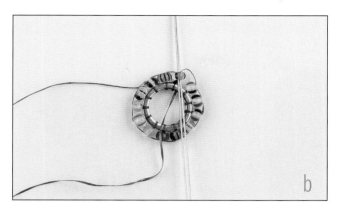

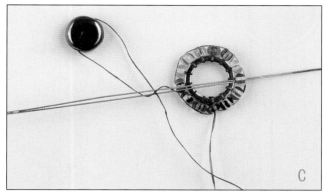

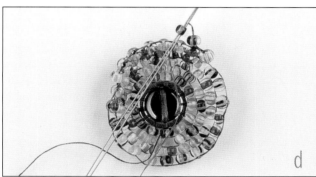

**3** | Continue working in circular brick stitch. The remaining rounds are worked in the traditional method. You will pass the needle under the thread bridge instead of under the frame. The second row is worked using 15A and the third row is worked using 20A. Weave in the thread ends and trim.

**4** | Repeat steps 1–3 to make another bottom half of a wing.

## MAKE THE TOP HALF OF THE WING

**NOTE:** *The tail of the top wing will be used to attach the D embellishment and then woven into place to add the points.*

**5** | Follow steps 1–3 using 3' of thread and leaving an 8" tail.

**6** | Work a fourth round using 22A.

**7** | Work two short rows. First work seven brick stitches. Weave the thread around so that it is exiting the sixth stitch. Work five brick stitches **(photo d)**. The short rows will be used when assembling the butterfly. Repeat steps 5–7 to make another top half of a wing.

## START ASSEMBLY

**NOTE:** *When stitching the wings together, remember they are mirror images of each other. The short rows worked on the top halves will be stitched together. Keep this in mind when sewing the bottom pieces to the top. You might need to use the big-eye collapsible needle to sew the wings together. Don't force the regular needle, or you might end up breaking a bead!*

# BONUS VERSIONS

For the pearl or crystal version of the butterfly, you can work round 1 following the instructions in the "Faux Circular Brick Stitch Earrings," p. 16 (steps 1–5) or work the traditional way shown in the "Circles in Time Earrings," p. 74. Both use a 6mm bead as the center bead. To complete these versions, follow the instructions for the butterfly. Keep in mind that even though the number of beads used to create the short rows varies, you'll sew them together the same way. Here are the stitch counts for the rounds/steps:

**Pearl Butterfly**
Work using 3mm pearls (the faceted puffy rondelle replaces the brick bead).
**Bottom half of wing (make 2):** Round 1, work 9. Round 2, work 13.
**Top half of wing (make 2):** Repeat steps 1 and 2 from above. Rounds 3–17, work a short row of 4.

**Blue Butterfly**
**Bottom half of wing (make 2):** Work 11 2mm seed beads. Work 13 3mm fire polished beads. Work 20 2mm seed beads.
**Top half of wing (make 2):** Repeat steps 1–3. Work 20 3mm fire polished beads. Work a short row of seven 2mm seed beads.

**8 | Stitch the top and bottom of the wings together:** Pass the needle into the piece through one bead and back out through the next bead. The bottom piece is attached under the short rows. Four beads from the bottom are sewed to the top **(photo e)**.

**9 | Stitch the left and right wings together:** Match up the shorts rows and stitch the right and left wings together **(photo f)**. (Sewing the lower half of the wings together is optional.)

## CREATE/ATTACH THE BODY AND HEAD

**10 |** The body is attached over the joined short rows of the wings. The needle should be exiting approximately 4mm from the top. **Start the body:** Pick up 1F. Sew down through the beading and back up through it. Pass through the F again **(photo g)**. **Start the head:** Pick up 1G, 1F, 5B, and 1C. Pass the needle back down through 5B, 1F, 1G and 1F **(photo h)**. Pull thread so that there is no space between the beads. Now pick up another F for the body. Sew down and up through the beading. Pass through the first F added for the body and pass through the second hole of G. Complete the head. Pick up 1F, 5B, and 1C. Pass back through the 5B, 1F, 1G and 2F. **Finish the body:** Pick up 1F, 3E, and 1B. Pass back up through 3E, 3F, 1G, and 1F. Weave the working thread around to reinforce and then trim it.

**11 | Add points to top of wings at eleven o'clock and two o'clock:** The placement is about seven beads from center. Choose the spot based on what looks best to your eye. Your stitch spacing and the beads you used could impact the placement. Weave the tails of the top half into place. Pick up 3A and pass the needle into the next bead. Repeat on the other wing. Weave in the thread ends and trim.

**12 | Attach the pin back:** Open the pin back and center it on the back of the butterfly. Attach a new thread, and weave the thread through the beads to exit near a hole at one end of the pin back. Pick up 3A and pass through the pin to the right side of butterfly. Pass through one or two beads and to the back of the butterfly on the opposite side of the same pinhole. Pick up 3A and pass through the same pinhole to the front of the butterfly. Repeat to secure each hole of the pin back, passing through beads as needed to avoid exposing any bare thread. If the pin back feels wobbly, weave through the beads again to reinforce.

# Indian Fabric-Inspired Bracelet

## MATERIALS

*The bracelet is 7¹/₂" long, including the clasp.*

- 7g 2mm Japanese seed beads (bead A)

- 7g 2mm Japanese seed beads (bead B)

- hank 11º Czech seed beads (bead C)

- hank 11º Czech seed beads (bead D)

- hank 11º Czech seed beads (bead E)

- **24** 6mm round pressed glass beads (bead F)

- **24** 6mm flat squares (bead G)

- **24** 4mm glass pearls (bead H)

- toggle clasp

- beading thread, diameter 00.20 (.008")

## TOOLS

- scissors

- big-eye needle

Through this project you will get to apply what you learned about the circular brick stitch. In the introduction to the earring project, I mentioned that one of the uses of this stitch is that it could be used as part of a larger project. You will get to experience this aspect of the stitch by making this bracelet.

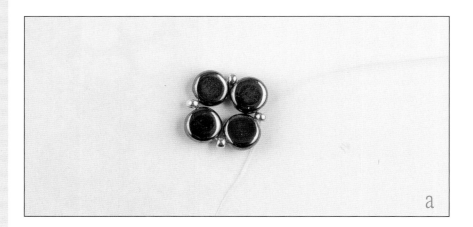

## MAKE THE BRACELET

**NOTE:** *The starter bead is the bead the thread is exiting at the beginning of the step.*

### MAKE THE DIAMOND COMPONENT

**1 |** Thread a needle on 2¹/₂' of thread. Pick up 1A, 1F, 1A, 1F, 1A, 1F, 1A, and 1F, leaving an 8" tail. Pass through all the beads again, tie an overhand knot, and pass through the first A again **(photo a)**.

**2 | Make the corners:** Pick up 3A, pass through the bead the thread was exiting at the start (starter bead), all 4A that make up the corner, the starter bead, the next F, and the next A **(photo b)**. Repeat three times. Step up by passing through the first corner A from the previous step and the first 2A added.

**3 | Add four squares:** Pick up 1G and pass through the top (outside) A in the next corner **(photo c)**. Repeat a total of four times. Repeat the thread path until secure. Weave the thread so it is exiting a G.

**4 | Embellish the corners with pearls:** Pick up 1A, 1H, and 1A, and pass through the next G **(photo d)**. Repeat three times. Pass the needle through all of the beads again a couple of times to tighten the tension. Weave the thread ends in and trim.

### MAKE THE CIRCLE COMPONENT

**NOTE:** *The number of beads used may vary, based on the bead size. The goal is for the beads to be evenly spaced around*

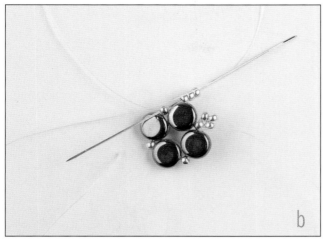

*the center bead. The instructions below are for the first row of the orange/red component. You will make five components in each color combination.*

**5** | Thread a needle on 3' of thread, and pick up 1F. Pass through the center twice and place one loop on each side. The stitches that surround the center coin bead will be worked off of these loops.

**6** | Every row of the brick stitch starts with two beads. For the first row, pick up 2C. Pass the needle under the thread loop (heading towards you) and up through the second bead. Pull the thread so the beads rest snugly on the center bead. (You may need to use your fingers to nudge the beads into place.)

**7** | Pick up 1C, pass the thread under the loop, and pass back up through the bead. Repeat all the way around until you have worked a total of 11 or 12 beads. (The number may vary.) After you complete the last stitch, pass down through the first bead, out toward the back, under the thread loop in front of the first bead, and through the first bead.

**8** | Continuing to work in brick stitch, follow steps 6 and 7 to make two additional rows using 14D and 19–20A.

**9** | Work three more stitches using As. These beads will be used to connect the components.

## ASSEMBLE
**NOTE:** *You will have to add thread and weave in ends throughout the assembly process.*

**10** | **Connect two circle components (one of each color combination) to two diamond components:** Your needle should be exiting the last stitch worked on a circle component. Pass through a pearl bead of a diamond component, and then weave through the beads of the second circle. Weave in such a way that the needle is exiting the third A. Pass through the pearl of the second diamond. Complete the circuit by weaving through the first circle and ending up with the needle exiting an A that is three beads above the last 3A worked **(photo e)**. Each diamond component has two pearls on the outside edge. They will be attached to the circles on that side. Pick up 3A and pass through

the closest pearl **(photo f)**. Continue connecting the remaining pieces working the same way, alternating the placement of the circle color combinations.

**NOTE:** *All the outside pearls are attached to the circles. Use the thread from both circles to connect and reinforce the connections.*

**11 | Attach the clasp:** Attach a new thread to the pearl at one end. Pick up 8A, and pass through an H from the opposite direction and the first 4A picked up. Pass through the loop of the clasp, the last 4A picked up, and the H. Retrace the thread path until secure **(photo g)**. Weave in the thread ends and trim. Repeat with the other half of the clasp.

# *Peyote Stitch*

# *Sparkling Mosaic Ring*

The most common metaphor used to describe the peyote stitch is the zipper. As you know, a zipper has teeth and when closed, they interlock. Instead of teeth, the peyote stitch has beads. The way beads are added to work the peyote stitch makes the piece resemble an open edge of a zipper. To turn the strip of beads into a ring band, you will have to join the ends together, which is called zipping it closed.

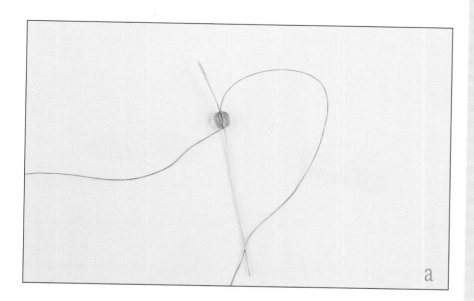

a

## MAKE THE RING

**NOTE:** *The band is created by working in an even-count, flat peyote stitch. Even-count means that the number of beads initially strung can be divided by two.*

## MAKE THE BAND

**NOTE:** *The group of beads picked up in the first step are often counted as the first two rows, and the first row worked in the peyote stitch is counted as the third row.*

**1 |** Thread a needle on a 4' piece of thread. Pick up the stop bead and pass through it again a couple of times, going in the same direction **(photo a)**. Pick up 4A.

## MATERIALS

- 2g 10º Czech seed beads (bead A)

- **18** 2mm Japanese seed beads (bead B)

- **1** two-hole Tila bead (bead C)

- beading thread, diameter 00.20 (.008")

## TOOLS

- scissors

- big-eye needle

## About Stop Beads

A stop bead (also called a stopper bead) is a temporary bead that is used to prevent project beads from falling off the thread. You can use any bead as a stop bead. I recommend choosing one that won't be confused with the project beads—use a bead a few sizes larger in a contrasting color.

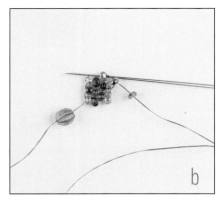

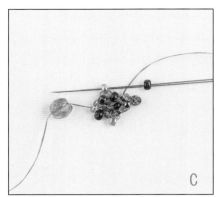

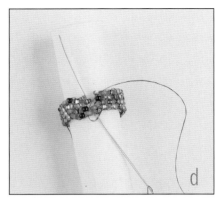

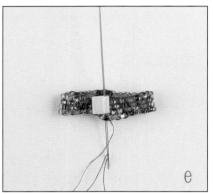

**2 |** (To make it easier to see the stitch, I worked a few rows already.) Pick up 1A, skip the first A, and pass through the next A **(photo b)**.

**3 |** Pick up 1A, skip 1A, and pass through the last A **(photo c)**.

**4 |** Continue working in peyote stitch as in steps 1 and 2, reversing direction with each row, until the band is long enough to fit comfortably around your finger.

**5 | Zip the ends together:** Fold the ring so the ends meet in the middle. If the first bead on one end is an up-bead, then the corresponding spot at the other end should be a down-bead. In other words, the bead at the ends of your piece should fit together like the teeth on a zipper. Remember, you aren't picking up any new beads, but rather passing through beads from the other end as if you had picked them up. You will be moving the needle in a zig-zag fashion. Repeat the path going in the opposite direction **(photo d)**.

**NOTE:** *You might have to add or subtract a row in order for the ends to interlock.*

## ADD THE FOCAL COMPONENT
**6 | Attach the C to the band:** Pick up 1C, pass through the band following the stitch path, and then go

back through the C again **(photo e)**. Repeat several times until secure. Then repeat with the second hole.

## CREATE THE TILA BEAD FRAME
**7 |** Pick up 4B and pass through the hole on the opposite side **(photo f)**. Pass through all 4B again.

**8 |** Pick up 2B and pass through the second hole **(photo g)**.

**9 |** Pick up 4B and pass through the hole on the opposite side.

**10 |** Pick up 2B, and pass through the second hole and the 2B (the fifth and sixth) picked up on the other side.

**11 | Fill in the open spaces of the frame:** Pick up 2B and pass through the group of four along the side.

**12 |** Pick up 2B and pass through the next two beads.

**13 |** Pick up 1B and pass through the four beads along the side. Pick up 1B and pass through the four along the top.

**14 |** Pass through all the Bs until secure. You can also pass through the C while securing the frame. Weave the tail ends in and trim.

# Flirty Girl Bracelet

## Practice

## MATERIALS

*The bracelet is 7" long, including the clasp.*

- **7g** 15º Japanese seed beads (bead A)

- **1** hank 11º Czech seed beads (bead B)

- **1** hank 10º Czech seed beads (bead C)

- **1** hank 8º Czech seed beads (bead D)

- **34** 6mm fire-polished beads (bead E)

- **40** 6mm flat square beads (bead F)

- **1** 16mm rivoli

- beading thread, diameter 00.20 (.008")

## TOOLS

- big-eye needle

- scissors

In the first peyote project, you learned the basic flat, even-count peyote stitch. In this project, you'll practice it while making the bracelet band. The focal component is created by making a beaded bezel using tubular peyote stitch for the rivoli. A bezel is just a fancy cup. Tubular peyote is very similar to regular peyote. The primary difference is that at the end of a row, you step up by sewing through the first up-bead added in the round.

## MAKE THE BEADED BEZEL

**NOTE:** *You may need to adjust the number of beads used due to the type of beads you use and your tension. It will be easier to make a beaded bezel with quality beads that have a consistent size and shape. In order for the bezel to hold the rivoli, the second bead used must be a full size smaller. How tightly you pull the thread for each stitch can impact the number of beads used.*

**1** | Thread a needle on 3' of thread. Pick up 36C or enough even-count of beads to fit around the circumference of the rivoli, leaving an 18" tail. Form a ring by passing through all the beads again and the first bead **(photo a)**. Pick up 1C, skip 1C, and pass through the next C **(photo b)**. Continue working in tubular peyote stitch to complete the round, and step up by passing through the first C added **(photo c)**. Work a second round of peyote stitch using Cs.

**2** | Work the next two rounds in tubular peyote stitch using As. Keep the tension tight to decrease the size of the ring and create your bezel.

**3** | Position the rivoli face down in the bezel cup. Using the tail thread, work three rounds using As **(photo d)**.

## MAKE THE BRACELET BAND

**4** | Thread a needle on 3' of thread. Pick up a stop bead, leaving a 6" tail. Pass through the bead again. Pick up 1E, 1F, 1E, 1F, 1E, 1F, 1E, and 1F.

**5** | **Make a square bead row:** Pick up 2B and 1F. Skip the first bead and pass through the next. Peyote

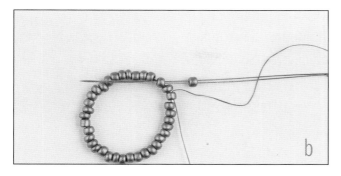

b

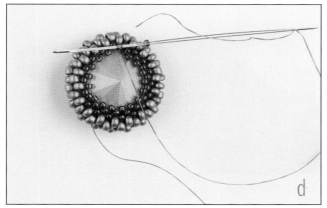

d

c

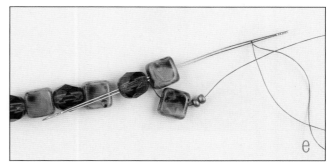

e

f

g

stitch using 1F for the rest of the row **(photo e)**.

**6 | Make an E row:** Pick up 3B and 1E. Skip the first bead and pass through the next. Peyote stitch using 1E for the rest of the row.

**7 |** Repeat steps 5 and 6 twice and step 5 for the third time. (You will have worked a total of five rows.) Remove the stop bead.

**8 | Fill in the spaces using Ds:** Pick up 1D. Pass down through the E and all the beads below and exit on the opposite end. Pick up 1D and pass through the next 2B; repeat four times. Pick up 1D. Pass down through the F and all the beads below, exiting at the other end. Pick up 1D and pass through the next 3B; repeat three times. Step up by passing through the first D added in this step. Repeat steps 4–8 to create a second band.

## CREATE CONNECTORS:
**9 | Begin creating the first end:** Pick up 2C and pass through the next D. Repeat two times **(photo f)**.

**10 |** Pick up 1D and pass it through the 2C. Repeat two times.

**11 |** Pick up 1D and 1C and pass through the next D. Pick up 1C and pass through the next D. Repeat **(photo g)**.

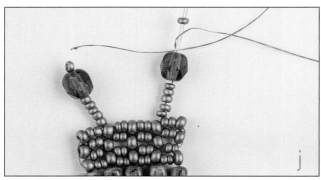

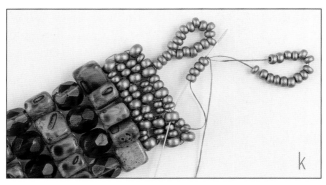

**12 |** Work two more rows in peyote stitch using 1C per stitch.

**FINISH THE CLASP END**

**13 |** The second side is worked using the tail. Weave it to the other side. The thread should pass through the end D from inside edge to outside edge. Pick up 2C and pass through the next D. Repeat four times.

**14 |** Pick up 1D and pass through 2C. Repeat four times **(photo h)**.

**15 |** Pick up 1D and 2C. Pass through D. Pick up 2C and pass through the next D; repeat three times.

**16 | Complete the second band:** Repeat step 13. In preparation for the next row, pass through the closest D from a previous step. Repeat step 14.

## ASSEMBLE

**17 | Attach the bands to the focal component:** The technique is similar to the one used in the ring project. Instead of zip stitching the ends of

the ring band together, you will pass the needle back-and-forth between the band and the focal component. Attach the band to the outside edge of the beaded bezel. To make the connection strong, repeat the path several times. Weave in the thread and trim the ends **(photo i)**.

**18 | Create clasp components:** The clasp components are worked off of the second and fourth D of the band ends. **Make the 6mm bead side:** Weave the thread so it is exiting the second D. Pick up 5C, 1E, and 1C. Pass back down through the E and the 5C **(photo j)**. Pass through the starter bead so you are positioned to repeat the path. Retrace the thread path until it is secure. Repeat on the fourth D. Weave the thread ends in and trim.

**19 | Finish the loop side:** Weave the thread so it is exiting the second D. Pick up 19B. Pass down through the first 4Bs picked up **(photo k)**. Pass through the starter bead again from the opposite side. Your thread should be exiting the starter bead from the same side as you started. Retrace the thread path. Repeat on the fourth C. Weave the thread ends in and trim.

*Candy Wrapper Link Necklace*

## MATERIALS

*The necklace is 16³/₄" long, including the clasp.*

- 7g 1.5mm Japanese seed beads (bead A)

- 7g 2mm Japanese seed beads (bead B)

- 7g 3mm Japanese seed beads (bead C)

- 20 g 12º Japanese seed beads (bead D)

- **1** 14mm rivoli

- **1** 16mm rivoli

- **1** 18mm rivoli

- toggle clasp

- beading thread, diameter 00.20 (.008")

## TOOLS
- scissors

- big-eye needle

**NOTE:** *The links are about 1" long. Adding or subtracting a link on each end will make the necklace longer or shorter by approximately 2".*

# Bezel Hints
You may need adjust the number of beads used in your bezel due to the type and quality of seed beads you use and your tension. It will be easier to make a beaded bezel with quality beads that have a consistent size and shape. In order for the bezel to hold the rivoli, the second bead used must be a full size smaller. How tightly you pull the thread for each stitch (your tension) can impact the number of beads used as well.

To create the links in this piece, you'll use what you learned from the first project: basic, even-count peyote stitch. To create the focal component, you'll use what you learned from the second project: placing a rivoli in a bezel. Adjusting the length is easy—simply make as many links as you need!

## BEADED BEAD LINKS
**NOTE:** *Make 12 links or the number required to reach your desired length.*

**1 |** Thread a needle on a 3' piece of thread. Pick up a stop bead, leaving a 7" tail, and pass through it again. Pick up 1A, 1B, 10D, 1B, and 1A. Pick up 1A, skip the first bead, and pass through the second bead. Pick up 1D, skip one bead, and pass through the next D. Work a total of 5D. Pick up 1B and pass through the last A. Continue working in the same way using peyote stitch until you have worked 18 rows of peyote stitch. (This is in addition to the 14 beads originally strung that count as two rows.)

**2 | Turn the peyote strip into a tube:** Match up the two ends so that the rows fit together (like a zipper). Zip stitch together by sewing through the up beads on each end, alternating in a zigzagging pattern **(photo a)**. To complete and secure the ends, after exiting the last up bead, pass the needle down through the adjacent bead and continue weaving back and forth until you reach the other end.

**3 | Embellish the link ends:** Pick up 3C. Press the link between your thumb and pointer finger to flatten it to identify the bead opposite the starter bead. Pass the needle down through the corresponding bead on the opposite side and up through the closest bead. Reinforce the added beads by repeating the thread path a couple of times. The thread should be exiting the center bead. Repeat this embellishment on the other end using the tail. Make sure both ends match **(photo b)**.

## BEZEL SET THE RIVOLI
**NOTE:** *Follow the same process for creating a bezel for the three different-sized rivoli. The only difference is the number of beads used. You will pick up 38D for the 18mm crystal, 34D for the 16mm crystal, and 32D for the 14mm crystal.*

**4 |** Thread a needle on 3' of thread. Pick up 38D or enough even-count of beads to fit around the circumference of the rivoli. Form a ring by passing through all the beads again and the first bead. **Begin working the peyote stitch:** Pick up 1D, skip the next bead in the ring, and sew through the following bead. Continue working in tubular peyote stitch to complete the round, and step up by passing through the first bead added.

a

b

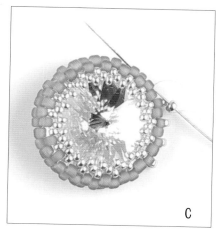

c

d

Work another row using D.

**5 |** Work the next three rounds in tubular peyote stitch using A. Keep the tension tight to decrease the size of the ring. Weave the thread to the other side of the bezel.

**6 |** Position the rivoli face down in the bezel cup. Work three rounds of peyote using A.

**7 | Embellish the outer edge:** Work the thread so it is exiting a bead along the outside edge of the rivoli. Using Bs, work one row of tubular peyote **(photo c)**. The second embellishment row is worked when you assemble the necklace.

## ASSEMBLE

**8 |** Make two chains of six links. Thread should be exiting the center C used to embellish the link ends. Pick up 1C, pass through the corresponding C in the next link, pick up 1C, and pass through the starter bead. Make the connection between the links secure by repeating the thread path through all four Cs **(photo d)**. Weave the thread end in and trim. Repeat four more times, creating a chain made of six links.

**NOTE:** *The key to lining up the three crystals is the middle crystal. The number of Cs used to fill in the spaces must be the same on the right and the left side. Adjust accordingly.*

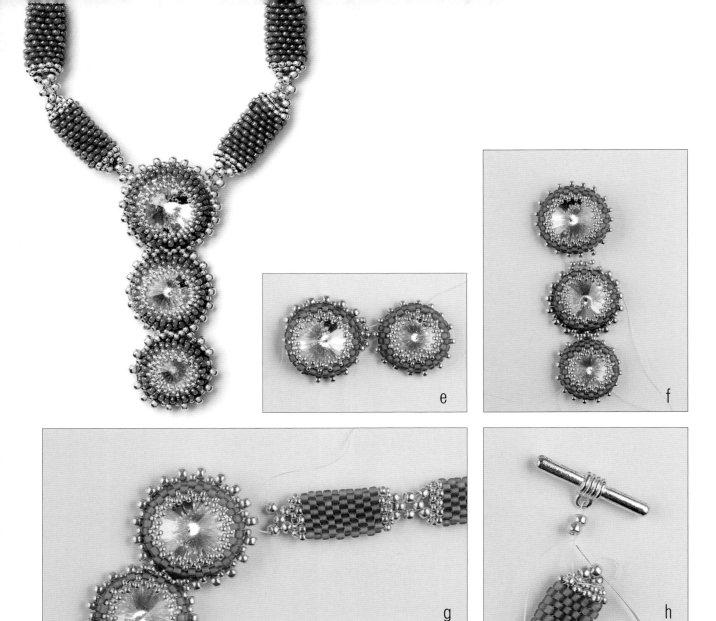

e

f

g

h

**9 | Join the rivolis together to create the focal component:** Pick up 1B and zigzag between the Bs used to embellish their outside edge. Thread should be exiting a B used to embellish the medium crystal. Pick up 1C and pass through the next B. Fill in six spaces using Cs. [Pick up 1 B and pass through the small crystal's B. Pick up 1B and pass through the medium crystal's B.] Repeat the instructions between the brackets **(photo e)**. Fill in the next six spaces using 1B per space. Repeat to connect the medium crystal to the large crystal. Fill in all the remaining spaces of the three crystals with 1C per space. Weaving thread ends in strengthens the connection points among the crystals **(photo f)**.

**10 | Attach the chains to the largest bezel-set rivoli:** The method is the same as connecting links together. Starting at the bottom of the large crystal,

count up 6C. Attach a chain to the sixth C on each side. Pick up a chain. The thread should be exiting a center C. Pick up 1C, pass through the sixth C from the large crystal, pick up 1C, and close the circuit by passing through the original C. Repeat the path until secure **(photo g)**. Weave in the thread end and trim. Repeat with the second chain.

**11 | Attach the clasp:** The thread should be exiting the center C at the unattached end of the strand. Pick up 2C and half of the clasp, pass through the second C picked up, and pick up 1C. Pass through the C from the strand so that you are back at the starting point. Retrace the thread path until secure **(photo h)**. Weave in the thread end and trim. Attach the other half of the clasp in the same way to the other strand.

# Combined Stitches

### SQUARE STITCH & PEYOTE STITCH
# Pentagon Tanzanite Bracelet

This project gives you the opportunity to make a bracelet that features two different bead stitches: square stitch and peyote stitch. They come together beautifully in a gorgeous bracelet.

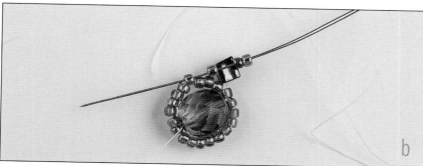

**NOTE:** *The starter bead is the bead the thread is exiting at the start of a step.*

## LINKS

**NOTE:** *Work steps 1–8 to make a starter link and then make six links by working steps 1–7.*

**1 | Frame the focal bead:** Thread a needle on 3½' of thread. Pick up 1D (the focal bead) and 10A, leaving a 6" tail. Pass through the D, 10A, and the D. Pick up 10A. Pass through the D, 10A, and the D. Close the gap between the two sides of the frame by passing through all 20A and the first A picked up.

**NOTE:** *A long tail makes it easier to tighten up the tension on the beads closest to the focal D.*

**2 | Add five Cs and make five 4A units:**
[Pick up 1C, skip 3A, and pass through the fourth A **(photo a)**. Pick up 3A. Pass through the starter bead **(photo b)**]. Repeat this pattern a total of five times. Step up by passing through the first C picked up and the next 2A. The needle should be exiting the top A.

## MATERIALS
*The bracelet is 7½" long, including the clasp.*

- 2g 12° Japanese seed beads (bead A)

- 5g 12° Japanese seed beads (bead B)

- **35** 4mm cube beads (bead C)

- **7** 8mm round fire-polished beads (bead D)

- toggle clasp

- beading thread, diameter 00.20 (.008")

## TOOLS
- scissors

- big-eye needle

**COUNT YOUR BEADS**
*Be sure to count your beads as you go, so you don't have to undo work later. This is especially important in steps 1, 4, and 5 of this project.*

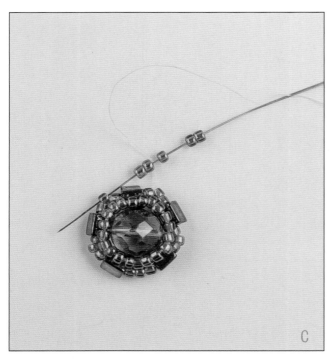

**3 | Create bead groups of 5A:** Pick up 5A and pass through the top A of the next four bead unit. Repeat all the way around. Weave your thread so it is exiting the last bead of a 5A group and pull to tighten up the tension of the beads added in this step **(photo c)**.

**4 | Using As, work 30 square stitches:** The 30 stitches are comprised of the 5A groups added in the previous step and the top A of the four bead units. Pick up 1A. Pass through the A bead directly below and through the A just picked up **(photo d)**. Repeat all the way around. Connect the last and first stitches worked by passing the needle through the beads of the first stitch, following the original thread path. Weave the thread through the last stitch worked, exiting the very last bead added.

**5 |** In this step, the needle passes through the first, third, and fifth bead of each five-bead group. Pick up 3B. Skip one A and pass through the next A bead (first corner started) **(photo e)**. Pick up 1B. Skip an A and pass through the next A. Pick up 1B, skip an A, and pass through the next A. Repeat this all the way around. Step up by passing through the first B of the first 3B group added.

**6 |** Pick up 2B and pass through the third bead of the group **(photo f)**. Work three peyote stitches. Repeat all the way around. Step up by passing through the first bead of the first pair added in this step.

**7 | Complete the starter link:** Finish the corners by working 1B (corner bead) between a pair of Bs **(photo g)** and working four peyote stitches along the sides.

## ASSEMBLE

**8 |** Zip stitch a link to the starter link. Match up the two links so that the sides fit together (like a zipper). Zip together by sewing through the up beads on each link, alternating in a zigzag pattern. The thread should be exiting between a pair of Bs on the link that is going to be attached. Pass through the corner bead of the starter link and then through the second bead of the pair of the attaching link, and continue zipping the sides together **(photo h)**.

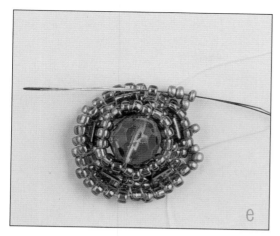

**9 | Complete the remaining sides of the attached link:** Using B, work four peyote stitches along the sides and one B between pairs. Weave in the ends and trim.

**10 |** Attach and complete the remaining links as described above.

### ATTACH THE CLASP

**11 | At each end of the bracelet, create a clasp connector strip off the outside corner bead:** Weave the thread to exit the bead before the corner bead. Pick up 1B and pass through the corner bead. Pick up 1B and pass through the next bead. Continue working along the peyote strip. For the ring side of the clasp, work a total of three rows; for the bar side, work a total of eight rows.

**12 | At each end of the bracelet, create a clasp connector strip:** The clasp connector is worked off of three beads (the bead before a corner, the corner bead and the bead after the corner bead. Weave or add thread so that the needle is exiting a B before the 3B described. Work three peyote stitches. Pick up 1B and pass through the next B. Repeat three times. For the ring side of the clasp, work a total of six rows; for the bar, work a total of ten rows.

**13 | Attach the clasp components to the clasp connectors:** Weave the thread to exit the center bead. Attach the clasp by sewing through its loop and back through the center bead. Retrace the path until secure. Weave the ends in and trim.

### LADDER AND PEYOTE STITCH

## *Corset Bracelet*

There is a twist to this stitch combination project. You'll work ladder stitch, but the stitch thread path for a two-hole Tila bead is different from that of a single-hole bead. Two-hole beads require an extra step to work in ladder stitch, which means the starting point for each stitch is the same.

## MATERIALS

*The bracelet is 7½" long, including the clasp.*

- 20g 12º Japanese seed beads (bead A)

- 7g 1.5mm Japanese seed beads (bead B)

- **64** two-hole Tila beads (bead C)

- **1** 16mm rivoli (bead D)

- toggle clasp

- beading thread, diameter 00.20 (.008")

## TOOLS

- scissors

- big-eye needle

### CONSTRUCTION NOTE

*The creation of the bracelet band can be broken into three parts. First, you'll make two bands comprised of Tila beads worked in ladder stitch. Tila beads are flat, square beads that have two holes. An additional step is required when working the ladder stitch using a two-hole bead. The needle has to go through the second hole in order to attach the next bead. The second part is embellishing the outside edges of the bands. The third part is connecting the two bands together.*

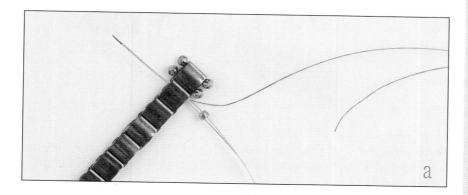

a

## MAKE THE BRACELET BAND

**NOTE:** *Make two strands of 32 Tila beads working in ladder stitch. Steps 1–3 apply to both top and bottom bands. The strands should be worked with tight tension, meaning there should be no visible space between the Tila beads. I recommend repeating the thread path twice for each bead added.*

**1 |** Thread a needle on the longest piece of thread on which you are comfortable working. Pick up 2C, and pass through the beads again. Remember to work with a tight tension. Pass through the second hole of the second bead.

**2 | Subsequent beads are added one at a time:** Pick up 1C. Pass up through the previous bead's second hole and down through the first hole of the bead just added. Pass up through the second hole of the added bead. Repeat until the band is made up of a total of 32C. The thread should be exiting the last hole of the strand.

### EMBELLISH THE STRANDS

**NOTE:** *The needle should only pass once through the seed beads that directly embellish the top and bottom of the C strand.*

**3 |** Pick up 1A, pass back down through the same hole you just exited, pick up 1A, and pass through the same hole. Pass through the second hole of the C **(photo a)**. Repeat along the entire length of the C strands. The thread should be exiting through the inside edge of an A at the end of the band.

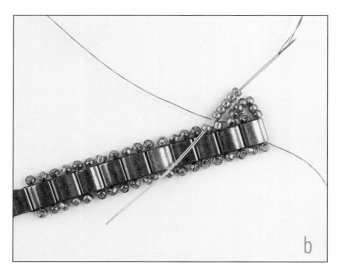

**4 | Add 5A groups to only one strand (strand 1):** Pick up 5A, skip one A, and pass through the next A **(photo b)**. Repeat all the way to the end of the band. Weave the thread around so it is exiting the inside edge of an A at the end of the strand.

**5 | Connect a second strand (strand 2) to strand 1:** Connect strand 2 to strand 1 by zigzagging back and forth from the odd-number beads and passing through the middle bead of the group of five beads on strand 1. The needle is exiting from the inside edge of the bead on strand 2. Pick up 2A, and pass through the the third bead of the 5A group from strand 1. Pick up 2A. Skip the second A on strand 2 and pass through the third bead **(photo c)**. Repeat all the way to the end.

## BEZEL SET THE RIVOLI

**6 |** Thread a needle on 3' of thread. Pick up 34A to fit around the circumference of the rivoli, leaving an 18" tail. Form a ring by passing through all the beads again. Pick up 1A, skip the next bead in the ring, and sew through the following bead. Continue working in tubular peyote stitch to complete the round, and step up through the first bead added.

**7 |** Work the next two rounds in tubular peyote using Bs. Keep the tension tight to decrease the size of the ring.

**8 |** Position the rivoli in the bezel cup. Using the tail thread, work one round of tubular peyote along the other side using As and then two rounds using Bs.

## ASSEMBLE

**9 | Attach the focal component:** Place the bezel-set rivoli in the middle of the band, sew into place, weave the ends in, and trim.

**10 | Attach the clasp:** The thread should be exiting from the middle bead of the center section. To attach the bar end of the clasp, pick up 4A. Pass through half of the clasp, go back through the 4A just added, and pass through the starter bead again. Retrace the thread path until secure. Weave in the thread ends and trim. Repeat on the opposite side for the ring side of clasp, only picking up 2A.

Apply

Explore these sections before making this necklace: Ladder, Square, and Brick. In the instructions, I note which stitches are used where, and how I've made modifications.

## MATERIALS

*The necklace is 16" long, including the clasp.*

- 14g 2mm Japanese seed beads (bead A)

- 7g 1.5mm Japanese seed beads (bead B)

- 7g 3mm Japanese seed beads (bead C)

- **1** 8mm fire-polished bead (bead D)

- **25** 4mm round pearls (bead E)

- two-strand box clasp

- beading thread, diameter 00.20 (.008")

## TOOLS
- big-eye needle

- scissors

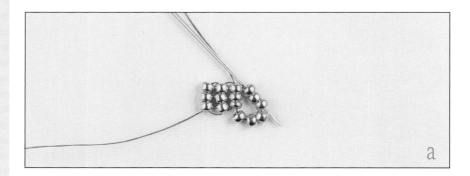

## MAKE THE CENTER SECTION

**NOTE:** *The center is worked in a modified ladder stitch. In standard ladder stitch, you pass through all the beads. You will not pass through every bead in this modification. The necklace band can be broken into three parts: center, top, and bottom. The center, which begins and ends with two three-bead columns, is completed first.*

**1 |** Thread a needle on the longest piece of thread on which you are comfortable working. **Create two columns of 3A:** Pick up 6A. Pass up through the first 3A and down through the next 3A.

**2 |** Pick up 3A, pass down through the previous column and up through the 3A just added.

**3 | Make a six-bead loop:** Pick up 6A, pass up through the previous column and down through the first 3A just added **(photo a)**.

**4 | Add two more 3A columns:** Pick up 3A, and pass down through the first 3A from the previous step and up through the 3A just added **(photo b)**. Work another 3A stitch.

**5 | Make an eight-bead loop:** Pick up 8A, and pass down through the previous column and up through the 8A added in this step.

**6 | Add two more 3A columns:** Pick up 3A, and pass up through the last 3A of the previous step and down through the 3A just added. Work another 3A stitch.

**7 | Make an eight-bead loop:** Pick up 8A, and pass up through the previous column and down through the first 3A just added.

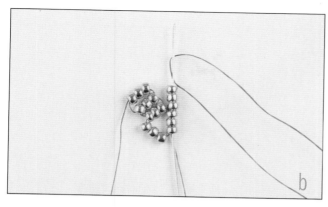

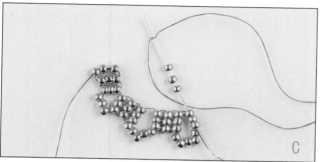

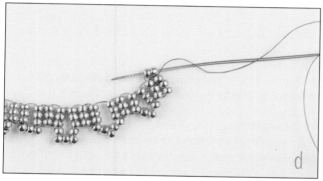

**8 | Add two more 3A columns:** Pick up 3A, pass down through the first 3A added in the previous step and up through the 3A just added **(photo c)**. Work another 3A stitch.

**9 | Make a six-bead loop:** Pick up 6A, and pass down through the previous column and up through the 6A added in this step.

**10 | Add two more 3A columns:** Pick up 3A. Pass up through the last 3A added from the previous step and down through the 3A just added. Add another 3A column.

**11 | Make an eight-bead loop:** Pick up 8A, pass up through the previous column and down the first 3A just added.

**12 | Add two more 3A columns:** Pick up 3A, pass

down through the first 3A added in the previous step and up through the 3A just added. Work another 3A stitch.

**13 | Make an eight-bead loop:** Pick up 8A, and pass down through the previous column and up through the 8A just added.

**14 | Add two more 3A columns**: Pick up 3A, pass up through the last 3A added of the previous step and down through the 3A just added. Work another 3A stitch.

**15 |** Repeat steps 3–13 nine times.

## MAKE THE TOP SECTION
**NOTE:** *The first stitch of the top section should be worked over the first stitch of the middle. To begin, the thread should be exiting the top edge of an end bead.*

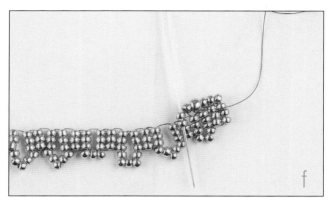

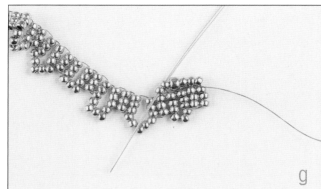

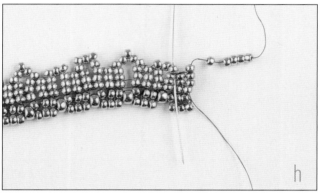

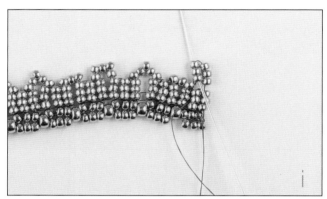

**16 |** Pick up 2A, and pass down through the second A from the end, up through the first A and through the 2A just added **(photo d)**.

**17 |** Pick up 1A, 1C, and 1A. Skip the first A. Pass down through the second A, up through the first A, and through the beads added in this step **(photo e)**.

**18 |** Pick up 1A, and pass down through the A below, up through the previous A and pass through the A above and the A just added **(photos f and g)**.

**19 |** Repeat steps 17 and 18 all the way to the end until there is one bead left.

**20 |** Pick up 1A, and pass down through the A below, up through the previous A, and through the A above and the A just added.

**21 | Now, reverse direction and work back along the row you just made:** Pick up 1A. Pass back through the A bead directly below it and through the A bead just added. Work three square stitches and pass the needle through the next C. Repeat to the end.

## BOTTOM SECTION

**NOTE:** *This section is worked in a modified brick stitch—like the standard brick stitch, except the needle goes under the bridge and it* goes up through three beads instead of one. To begin, exit the first column of 3A (the side with a 6A loop).

**22 |** Create two columns of 3A. Pick up 6A, pass the needle under the bridge that precedes the six-bead loop, and pass back up through the last 3A added as if it were one bead in standard brick stitch **(photos h and i)**.

**23 |** Pick up 1A, 1E, and 4A. Pass under the bridge that precedes the next eight-bead loop and pass back up through the last 3A added **(photo j)**.

**24 |** Pick up 10A. Pass under the bridge that precedes the next eight-bead loop and back up through the last 3A added. Repeat **(photo k)**.

**25 |** Pick up 10A. Pass under the bridge that precedes the next six-bead loop and back up through the last 3A added.

**26 |** Repeat steps 23–25 to the end. **There is slight modification regarding the last 10A picked up:** Pass the needle under the bridge after the last 8A loop and pass through the last 3A picked up. Pick up 3A and pass the needle through 3A at the end.

## FOCAL COMPONENT

**27 |** Thread a needle on 4' of thread. Pick up 1D and

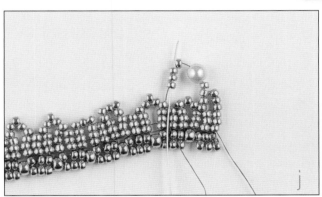

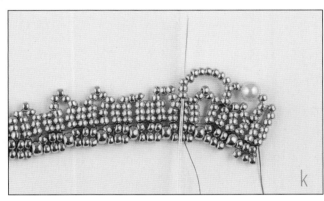

10A, leaving a 1' tail. Pass through 1D and 10A. Tie an overhand knot with a tail. Pick up 10A, and pass through 1D, 10A, and 1D. **Create a setting for the focal bead by working in square stitch:** Pick up 1A. Pass through the A directly below and through the bead that was just picked up. Work a total of 20 square stitches. **Connect the two ends by making a circular path through the beads of the first and last stitch:** Treat the beads of the first and last stitch as if they were one, and pass through the first bead worked as a stitch, the bead below it, and the one below the last stitched worked. Complete the path by passing through the beads added for the last stitch and the first stitch. Repeat this circular path a couple of times to secure.

**28 | Embellish with seven pearls:** Pick up 1B and 1E. Skip 2A and pass through the third A. Repeat for a total of six times. Pick up 1E. Pass through the first B and E added in this step.

**29 |** Pick up 2A and pass through the next pearl. Repeat seven times. Step up by passing through the first 2A picked up.

**30 | Work two square stitches between the pearls (into the beads added in the previous step):** Pick up 1A. Pass through the A below

and the one just picked up. Repeat for the second time and pass through the next E. Repeat all the way around. Reinforce the stitches by passing through the beads again, if necessary.

**31 |** Surround one pearl with 5A.

## ASSEMBLE

**32 |** Attach the focal component under the tenth pearl from the side that starts with a six-bead loop. The thread should be exiting the fourth of 5A. Pick up 3A, pass through the tenth pearl, pick up 3A, and pass through the 3A above the pearl (of the focal component) again. Repeat the thread path until secure. Weave in the ends and trim.

**33 | Attach the clasp:** Each half of the clasp is attached to one end of the necklace. Center the clasp on the necklace edge, and determine which beads are closest to the loops of the clasp. Attach a new thread, and weave the thread to exit one of those beads. Pass through the loop and complete the circuit by passing through the same bead. Repeat the thread path until secure. Exit the bead that would be closest to the second loop, and repeat to attach the second loop. Attach the other half of the clasp the same way. End the threads and trim.

# Acknowledgments

Thank you to friends and family for their enthusiasm and encouragement while I wrote this book.

I would like to express my appreciation to Bead Master for their generosity in providing materials for this book.

Thank you to the staff at Kalmbach Books: Erica Swanson, Associate Editor, who appreciated my designs and worked with me to develop and polish my artistic vision; Bill Zuback, whose photos make my work look beautiful; Lisa Schroeder, who created a lovely layout; and Dana Meredith, who completed the technical edit. Thanks again!

# About the Author

**Eve Leder** started her career as a published craft designer in 2010. A year later, her first published beaded jewelry project was featured on the cover. This inspired her to teach herself more about beading. Her work has appeared in over a dozen different publications: Bead Design Studio, Bead Unique, BeadWork, Crafts 'n things, Craft Ideas, Create and Decorate, Crochet World, Just Cards, PolymerCAFE, Quick and Easy Painting Rubber-StampMadness, Scrap and Stamp Arts, Soft Dolls and Animals, and Stitch. Her artistic expression can take many forms: beading, crocheting, decorative painting, decoupage, jewelry making, knitting, paper crafts, polymer clay, and sewing. She taught herself most of what she knows.

If you are interested in seeing more of her work, please visit her blog at *eveleder.com*.

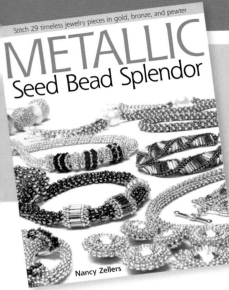
  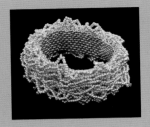